The Return of the Ripper?

The Return of the Ripper?

The Murder of Frances Coles

Kevin Turton

PEN & SWORD
TRUE CRIME

An imprint of
Pen & Sword Books Ltd
Yorkshire - Philadelphia

First published in Great Britain in 2023 by
Pen & Sword True Crime
An imprint of
Pen & Sword Books Ltd
Yorkshire - Philadelphia

ISBN 978 1 39906 470 5

Typeset in INDIA by IMPEC eSolutions
Printed and bound in England by CPI (UK) Ltd.

Pen & Sword Books Ltd incorporates the Imprints of Pen & Sword Archaeology, Atlas, Aviation, Battleground, Discovery, Family History, History, Maritime, Military, Naval, Politics, Railways, Select, Transport, True Crime, Fiction, Frontline Books, Leo Cooper, Praetorian Press, Seaforth Publishing, Wharncliffe and White Owl.

For a complete list of Pen & Sword titles please contact

PEN & SWORD BOOKS LIMITED
47 Church Street, Barnsley, South Yorkshire, S70 2AS, England
E-mail: enquiries@pen-and-sword.co.uk
Website: www.pen-and-sword.co.uk

or

PEN AND SWORD BOOKS
1950 Lawrence Rd, Havertown, PA 19083, USA
E-mail: uspen-and-sword@casematepublishers.com
Website: www.penandswordbooks.com

Contents

PART FOUR: THE CANONICAL FIVE

Acknowledgements

Since embarking on this project, I have come into contact with a number of people who have helped, guided and aided in my research. Too numerous to name but I thank them all. I would also like to thank the Maritime History Archive – Newfoundland & Labrador who have been of great help in helping me research certain key individuals. I must also thank Maureen Yule for her research, patience, support and editing skills which have enabled this book to reach completion.

Introduction

This is the story of a murder that has baffled and confounded investigators for well over one hundred years. Its significance has been much debated and argued over by criminologists (both professional and amateur), historians, retired police officers, authors of true crime and any with an interest in the crimes of Jack the Ripper. Its location and place in time, Whitechapel, 1891, the cause of all this speculation.

For many, myself included, either it marks the continuation of a reign of terror that gripped London throughout the latter quarter of 1888, or it highlights the possible emergence of a previously unknown serial killer.

Everything about the murder of Frances Coles, a woman who fitted the victim profile of the Whitechapel killer, suggested the Ripper had returned. Newspaper headlines across the country supported this idea and the initial police investigation followed the protocols and procedures that had been laid down three years earlier. But for the family she was never a statistic. Whatever her lifestyle, however difficult her life had been, she was always more than just a victim of an unknown killer. For them perhaps the rumour and speculation surrounding the case, and its unfortunate unsought link with the murders of 1888, hindered the police investigation.

It certainly caused speculation across the country and drew letters and commentary from armchair detectives nationwide; it also raised a question no one wanted to answer; did the Whitechapel killer not stop after the murder of Mary Jane Kelly? The police, it seems, were uncertain, though some of its high-ranking officials believed he did not. A view it is fair to say, which was, in the main, shared by much of the press. Conjecture which has continued, despite the passing of more than a century. As a result, it ensured the Frances Coles case would never receive the scrutiny afforded to that of the much-publicised canonical five.

The Victorian police force, perhaps much maligned by its inability to get to grips with the Ripper killings, was never likely to solve any of the cases. Most murders at that time happened in the home, amongst the family, in a dispute or a street brawl where victim and attacker were never far apart. Serial killers were unheard of. So, for a local force of 473 constables, forty-four sergeants and thirty inspectors whose daily lives revolved around petty crime, murders of this magnitude were always likely to prove beyond their detecting capabilities. But they were learning.

Sir Arthur Conan Doyle's, *A Study in Scarlet*, had introduced Sherlock Holmes, the thinking man's detective, in 1887. A detective able and capable when it came to understanding the criminal mind, blessed with observation skills that would have been the envy of the world when he stepped on to the fictional, criminal stage. Erudite, perceptive, at times insufferable and always triumphant. A man designed by his creator to be almost the opposite of what modern policing was in the late 1880s, essentially forensic in his approach to crime.

In many ways, fictional though he was, he represented a changing view amongst many on the fringes of the legal and medical professions. Throughout the Victorian period, the science of crime, its detection and the role played by forensic pathology in understanding murder, had been changing. London's detective force had grown in size and stature since its inception back in 1842 to become a recognised, efficient body of plain clothes policemen with a burgeoning enviable reputation under Metropolitan Police Commissioner Sir Charles Warren by 1888. Though there had been difficulties along the way.

In the medical profession, where advances in post-mortem procedures and the collection of evidence gained had proved valuable, progress had perhaps been slower. But by the 1860s there was already greater understanding of the mechanics of how time of death could be calculated. Fingerprint technology and the science behind it was also developing and the notion that the crime scene itself had a story to tell was being better understood. All of which was being absorbed into the mind of Sherlock Holmes' creator and in turn being passed on to the public at large.

The problem for those involved in the Ripper murders throughout the 1880s was simply that this was all still in its infancy, and its importance some twenty-odd years away from being fully understood. So, in that respect, the Ripper, or the killers hidden beneath the umbrella of that infamous nickname were all extremely lucky. All murders in the years after 1888 up until around 1895, and a few prior to his August 1888 start date that were later revisited and added to the list, were deemed to have a touch of the Ripper about them, Frances Coles included. The question posed by this book is one that has been raised many times over the years. Was *she* the last victim?

The question is valid because there are no other similar murders after February 1891, unless you take the view that he simply moved away from London and transferred his murderous skills to another country. A viewpoint shared by some and not without merit. Jack the Ripper murders were reported as happening all over the world. Newspapers resurrected the killer's profile in cases as far afield as France, America, South America, Austria, Jamaica and no doubt countless others. Today, just as he was at the end of the nineteenth century, Jack the Ripper is the most famous killer in criminal history, and he sold newspapers.

Just how valid any of these claims are is, obviously, impossible to quantify. But in the case of Frances Coles, and, probably, Alice McKenzie who died eighteen months earlier, the speculation is justified but not necessarily easy to substantiate, depending on how the crimes supposedly carried out by one man are viewed in the twenty-first century. This Victorian killer probably has a number of different personas, which means he may well have been more than a one-man killing machine dominating Whitechapel. As the narrative following will show, he is a name. The man or men hiding beneath it are far more complex than perhaps history would have us believe.

Key Characters Involved in the Whitechapel Murders

Chief Inspector Donald Sutherland Swanson – Brought into the Jack the Ripper investigation by Police Commissioner Sir Charles Warren after the Annie Chapman murder. Promoted to superintendent in 1896. Died in 1924.

Superintendent Thomas Arnold – Involved in most of the Jack the Ripper murders. Died in 1907.

Detective Inspector Edmund Reid – Head of CID in Metropolitan Police's H Division in 1888. Died in 1917.

Detective Inspector Henry Moore – Took over as lead detective from Inspector Abberline in 1889. Died in 1918.

Inspector Frederick Abberline – In charge of H Division CID until 1887. Transferred to A Division in Whitehall then on to Scotland Yard. Brought back to H Division in 1888 as part of the Jack the Ripper investigation team. Promoted to chief inspector in 1890. Retired in 1892 and died in 1929.

Police Constable Ernest Thompson – Discovered the body of Frances Coles in Swallow Gardens and heard the footsteps of her killer walk away. He was stabbed to death in 1900.

James Thomas Sadler – Sailor believed by police to have been involved in the death of Frances Coles in 1891.

Frances Coles – London prostitute who hid her occupation from her family. Murdered 13 February 1891 and believed by some to have been Jack the Ripper's last victim.

Ellen Calanna – Probably not her real name. London prostitute who knew Frances Coles and claimed to have been the last person to have seen her alive.

Dr George Bagster Phillips – H Division police surgeon with a surgery in Spital Square.

Dr George William Sequeira – First doctor on the scene in Mitre Square after the discovery of the body of Catherine Eddowes.

Dr Frederick Gordon Brown – Police surgeon for the City Police

Dr Rees Llewellyn – Attended the scene of Mary Ann Nichols murder.

Dr Thomas Bond – Divisional surgeon for A Division who believed the canonical murder victims were all carried out by one man.

Dr Lyttelton Stewart Forbes Winslow – Psychiatrist who believed he knew the identity of Jack the Ripper.

Coroner Wynne Baxter – Presided over most of the Ripper inquests, including that of Frances Coles. Appointed coroner for the south-eastern division of Middlesex in 1886 on an annual salary of £2,208. He presided over 38,000 inquests and died in 1920 leaving an estate valued at £29,319.

Annie Millwood – Possibly a Jack the Ripper victim who survived an attack in February 1888.

Mary Ann Nichols – Considered first victim of Jack the Ripper, her body found in Bucks Row in August 1888.

Martha Tabram – Questionable but a possible Jack the Ripper victim. Believed by many to have been his first. She had been stabbed to death, her body found in George Yard Buildings, off Whitechapel Road in August 1888.

Annie Chapman – Considered the second victim, her body found in Hanbury Street in September 1888.

Elizabeth Stride – Considered the third, her body found in Berner Street in September 1888.

Catherine Eddowes – Considered the fourth, her body found in Mitre Square in September 1888.

Mary Jane Kelly – Considered the fifth and last victim, her body found inside a room in Miller's Court in November 1888.

Rose Mylett – Potential Jack the Ripper victim in December 1888, her body found in Clarke's Yard, off Poplar High Street in December 1888.

Alice McKenzie – Potential Jack the Ripper victim in July 1889, her body found in Castle Alley in July 1889.

Annie Chapman
29 Hanbury Street

Mary Ann Nichols
Buck's Row

Mary Jane Kelly
Miller's Court

Emma Smith
Osborn Street

Martha Tabram
George Yard

Alice McKenzie
Castle Alley

Elizabeth Stride
Dutfield's Yard

Catherine Eddowes
Mitre Square

Frances Coles
Swallow Gardens

Pinchin Street Torso
Pinchin Street

1888-1891 Whitechapel Murder Locations

● Indicates a Canonical Five Victim

Reynolds Map of London
(circa 1882)

PART ONE

MURDER

Chapter 1

The Discovery

It was the end of a long day for Kate McCarthy when her shift at the wine merchant's ended and she could make her way across Commercial Street and through the doors of the United Brothers Club. The premises sat opposite each other and working late afforded her an opportunity she would otherwise have missed: the chance to spend the evening with the club's night porter and the man she could well end up marrying, Thomas Fowler. Their meeting, usually around eight o'clock at night, had become a routine that allowed them time together and time alone later when Thomas walked her home to her parents' house on Royal Mint Street.

How late that would be generally varied; his job required him to stay until the club closed, but it was usually around midnight – though there were exceptions. One of them was 12 February, which had been a busier night than normal. By the time the two of them stepped out into the cold, it was around a quarter to one in the morning. It was a short walk to where Kate lived, taking about fifteen minutes, but it gave them time alone and no doubt a little privacy. Something hard to obtain and difficult to give up.

They stayed out in the cold in the shadow of the *Crown and Seven Stars* public house, which was almost adjacent to Kate's parents' home, until around a quarter to two in the morning. Kate later recalled that three men from the Great Northern Railway Depot had passed by on the opposite side of the road on their way to work just before she went indoors. She remembered checking the time by the wall clock once inside before making her way upstairs. Brothers Joseph and John Knapton, whom she knew reasonably well, had shouted 'good night' as they passed, and following them a minute or two later, William Friday whom she only knew by his nickname, 'Jumbo'.

There was nothing unusual in that. Royal Mint Street was a regular and well-used thoroughfare for men employed by the railway, either to gain access into the goods depots of the Great Eastern, Great Northern or the Midland railway companies, all of which occupied a large swathe of the northern side of the road, or to use the archway beneath the railway to pass from Royal Mint Street to Aldgate. Essentially it was a shortcut, used mainly to move goods and horses easily from one location to another. These three men, whom she knew to be carmen, working out of the GNR stables on Chamber Street, located at the other end of the central archway – Arch 45, or Swallow Gardens as it was known locally – were all headed in that direction. Thomas had agreed with Kate's recollection, though he thought the time to have been a little nearer two o'clock when the men passed, because he thought he had caught sight of a policeman walking a familiar beat in the opposite direction around the corner of Leman Street and remembered looking at his watch at about the same time. No one else, he was sure, had been on the street or passed by before or after the three railwaymen. Not that his attention was likely to have been focused on the street.

There was obviously far more to interest him at that time of night than just who was wandering about in the dark, and understandably so. However, the same could not be said of the three railmen. With only a long night's work to look forward to and a short walk to make, their observation skills ought to have been perhaps more finely tuned. The Knaptons were sure there had been no one else on the street that night and agreed with Thomas. But William Friday (Jumbo), who did not know where Kate McCarthy lived, later insisted he had seen a couple he did not recognise in a doorway as he walked towards Swallow Gardens: 'On my way to the stables, I saw a man and a woman standing in a doorway. I could not discern their faces distinctly but noticed that the woman wore a black hat.'

The couple he referred to in that doorway on Royal Mint Street were, he claimed, only about 50 or so yards from the turn that would take him down to Arch 45, the local Catholic school and the stables beyond. The time, he thought, was just after 1.45 a.m.

By this time, and some way behind him, the policeman Thomas Fowler had caught sight of reached the junction of Leman Street and Cable Street. One street below and out of sight, PC Ernest Thompson, on his first ever beat alone having only joined the force back in December, was four hours into a shift that had so far been routine. The beat he followed was essentially a loop. It took in only four streets: the whole of Chamber Street, which included the GNR stables and the archway at Swallow Gardens; a small section of Mansell Street, which gave access on to Great Prescott Street, a road running parallel to the start of his beat; then finally into a short section of Leman Street, between the Co-op office with its tall clock tower, and the corner of Chamber Street where he would begin the whole process again. A short beat that took around twenty minutes to complete.

PC Thompson's patrol was important for the local community and also the businesses that used Arch 45 to house building stock. Dimly lit by lamps at either end of its 40-yard length, and with a reputation amongst the police for being a favoured haunt of prostitutes, the archway itself also housed a narrow storage yard. This was well protected and hidden behind a wooden structure that occupied half its width and was secured by two locked doors, one each end of the arch. It was the constable's task throughout the night to check those doors were secure then return to Chamber Street and continue his beat. Something, despite the low-level light, he was able to do easily: 'If I were standing at the Chambers Street entrance, I should be able to see someone in the centre of the arch. You can see right through it at night; in the daytime it is not very light.'

According to his later statement, he was standing at the corner of Leman and Chamber Street, minutes after the railway men had passed. The time, by his reckoning, was around 2.15 a.m., confirmed by the Co-operative store's clock which he could see from where he stood. No doubt a usual night-time practice that helped gauge how long his beat was taking and check he was on schedule. At that point, he claimed to have heard footsteps ahead of him, unhurried, and walking, he believed, in the direction of Mansell Street about a couple of hundred yards or so further on. 'The sound was of someone walking ... I was about 80 yards off.'

At the time they caused him no concern. It was only as he reached the entrance into the Swallow Gardens arch that he realised just how significant those footsteps could have been.

Even without the use of his bullseye lamp, essentially an oil lamp hung from his belt, which had a round, magnified glass eye through which the emitted light was rendered considerably brighter, the body lying in the narrow road was easily discernible. Laid roughly central to the archway at around its darkest point, and despite the night-time shadow, it was not difficult to make out the form was that of a woman. She lay on her back, head towards him, feet pointing towards Royal Mint Street, one hand laid across her chest, the other at her side. A few feet from where she lay, he could see a hat in the road and a second hat close to the body. As he reached her and opened the lamp's lens, he could see she had been horrifically injured, though at that stage was not sure how. Blood had pooled around her head, there was what he thought to be a wound to her throat or neck and as he leaned in closer, he could see she was still alive, later stating: 'I saw her open and shut one eye.'

This was probably just the body shutting down because it appears he believed she was dead moments later. The blood loss had been too great. As he held the lamp closer, he could see how much of it had pooled around her head and shoulders, forming a long stream that ran freely away towards the gutter several feet away. At that point training kicked in. Deciding death had occurred was not his judgement to make. He simply followed the laid-down procedure, unfamiliar obviously at this early stage of his career, but one he had been recently coached to observe: Protect the scene, check the surrounding area, leave the body in situ, do not touch or move the clothing.

He then used his whistle to summon help. It arrived in the form of PC Frederick Hyde, who was on patrol in Royal Mint Street, some 250 yards away. He was joined within minutes by constables George Hinton, who had been patrolling nearby Cartwright Street, and George Elliot, who had been working as a plain clothes detective and on duty outside the Rothschild's refinery, not far from the main railway depot at the western end of Royal Mint Street, where he was keeping an eye on any foot traffic approaching from the Minories. Hyde quickly confirmed death and instructed Thompson to guard the body whilst he went off to find the nearest doctor. Hinton went back to Leman Street police station to fetch a senior officer as protocol demanded.

It only took about ten minutes for local doctor, Frederick Oxley, whom Hyde knew to be living nearest to the murder scene, to arrive. Living in nearby Dock Street meant he had been called on before and was familiar with the police procedure. Obviously, his examination, given the circumstances and poor light, was cursory but sufficient to confirm both Hyde's and Thompson's assessment that life was extinct, and the woman had died as a result of a violent attack, her throat cut in at least two places. The wounds, as far as he was able to ascertain, were so extensive that she would never have been able to survive the attack. Other than that, he made no further observations; although fully conversant with procedure and necessary protocols, murders were not his province. They fell, as he well knew, under the remit of the police's divisional surgeon and the various operational rules governing serious crime. So, after a brief consultation with the duty inspector, James Flanagan, who had arrived with PC Hinton whilst his examination had been ongoing, he stepped aside.

Flanagan had already organised for officers to be sent out to find Dr George Bagster Phillips, divisional surgeon, and bring him to the scene. After Dr Oxley had given him a brief, but reasonably concise report about the state of the victim's body, Flanagan pulled a small team together to begin a search of the archway. By this time, more officers had arrived at the murder site alerted by PC Thompson's whistle or having been sent by Leman Street police station, most of whom could be put to work searching the ground around the body, despite the poor light, to try and discover if the killer had left any evidence. They were much needed. The archway was not a simple, open structure, as PC Thompson knew all too well; its internal construction was complicated. It was well described by a reporter from the *Bristol Times and Mirror*:

> The place ... is little more than a passage through a railway arch, bordered on one hand by a brick wall springing into the roof, and on the other by a wooden hoarding which has been run up, cutting off quite two-thirds of the space under the arch, which is apparently used to store such rubbish as accumulates around a railway goods yard.
>
> ... So narrow is the passage that there is only just enough space between the hoarding on one side and the kerbstone on the other to permit one vehicle passing at a time, and even then the pedestrian has to keep close to the wall to avoid contact with the passing wheels. As regards light, the spot is very deficient, and in the middle of the passage, where the murder was committed, there is practically none.

All of which – and without the aid of good quality lighting – made the search difficult to conduct. But it did yield a single find. Approximately 18 yards from where the body lay, searchers found, lodged between a water pipe and a brick wall, two 1-shilling pieces wrapped in newspaper – scraps torn from the *Daily News* but without a date. Initial speculation was that they had fallen from the woman's hand or from a pocket in her dress, although Superintendent Thomas Arnold, who had arrived shortly after the discovery, doubted she had ever been in possession of the coins. He believed they originated from elsewhere, possibly hidden for an unknown purpose. What that purpose was is debateable, but looking at that find today suggests maybe the hiding place had perhaps been used as a bank, a place to deposit proceeds of theft; somewhere to leave money that could be retrieved at a later date. Certainly, in his later report Arnold dismissed the coins' importance to the investigation, and he was perhaps right. The discovery of 2 shillings was never going to name the killer.

But there were other avenues to follow: local inspector, Edmund Reid, arrived just as the search got underway and, in conjunction with Inspector Flanagan, organised those officers not involved in searching Arch 45 to begin a street search across the adjacent neighbourhood. In other words, pick up anyone still out on the streets at that time in the morning and have them questioned, the hope being there was still a chance the killer had not managed to escape indoors. Superintendent Arnold, who perhaps entertained a different view, had the scope of that search widened, because he felt that was exactly what he may have already done. The reasoning being, I suppose, that it was late, it was cold and there had by now been an increased police presence all around the area. Therefore, getting off the streets was as important as putting distance between killer and murder site. In light of how easily the Ripper had always managed to avoid the police throughout the late summer of 1888, this was a reasonable course of action. He instructed the team around him to include in their search as many of the various lodging houses, locally and scattered across Whitechapel, as was feasible. He wanted to know who had checked in after 2 a.m. and where. He also had telegrams sent to all divisions informing them of the murder so their own beat officers would be made aware. Clearly, he wanted no stone left unturned.

It was obviously a wise precaution to make, perhaps learnt from past mistakes. He no doubt knew just how quickly word on the street would spread once the sun came up and that would aid his case. It would also help create an ID because as divisional surgeon Dr Phillips, who arrived whilst all this was being organised, began his examination of the body no one knew who the victim was.

All they had at that point was a murdered woman, killed in the style of the Ripper, at an hour reminiscent of those past murders and by a method all too familiar. That method, confirmed by Dr Phillips at around 4.30 a.m., was three cuts to her throat not two. One from left to right, another from right to left and a third left to right again, all made, in his opinion, by a right-handed killer. However, as far as he could tell, given the poor light, there was no added mutilation to the body. They would have to wait until the post-mortem for anything more, which was, and is today, standard procedure.

But even without the autopsy results, and despite the doctor's statement, the killer in this case had not carried out any form of disfigurement. Superintendent Arnold knew full well there would be speculation around the circumstances of the woman's death. The question for him and his officers was simple enough and he knew the press would ask it. Has the Ripper returned?

Chapter 2

Identity

For most police officers there was probably no doubt. Any murder in Whitechapel using a knife, as was the case here, pointed a finger at the murders of 1888 and with good justification. There had been no definitive evidence to support the notion the serial killer of three years earlier had ever really gone away. Of course, there were theories. In fact, there had been an abundance of them, and from all quarters of English society. Some were credible, others less so, but all too often published by newspapers eager to keep the story alive and running. All of which led to a healthy scepticism amongst the public about the death, or disappearance of the Whitechapel killer, none of which helped make the area safer, or led to better protection for the women that still walked the streets at night selling sex.

It is probably safe to assume, therefore, when Superintendent Arnold left Swallow Gardens that morning, the Ripper, or the man behind that mask, was definitely on his mind. It was also likely to blight this investigation if he bought into the notion that the body beneath Arch 45 was another addition to the unsolved killing spree that had terrorised the area years earlier. Yet there was little choice. Thomas Arnold had been involved in all the Ripper murders and knew full well mutilation may have been a part of some, but not all. So, it would have been impossible to discount the idea that here was yet another killing with many of the hallmarks associated with the night-time killer of Whitechapel's prostitutes.

As dawn broke on 13 February, it is not hard to imagine a meeting taking place at Leman Street police station, H Division headquarters, to discuss that very idea. Chief Inspector Donald Swanson, considered by many to be one of the greatest detectives Scotland Yard had ever produced, had already arrived at the station. Accompanying him was another Ripper murder expert, Inspector Henry Moore, and, of course, Edmund Reid who had been at Swallow Gardens since the early hours. Reid was another genuine Ripper expert having joined H Division back in 1887 as a replacement for Frederick Abberline, a man whose name will forever be synonymous with Whitechapel and the murders of 1888. The presence alone of these three would probably have ensured such a meeting took place and there was much to discuss.

Speculation amongst most of the station's officers, who knew the dead woman simply as Frances, was that the victim was a working prostitute, just like every other Ripper victim. A fact probably not overlooked by either of the two senior officers. But at that stage they had no clear, confirmed official identity, which meant speculation was all it could be. Nevertheless, I have no doubt it influenced their thinking. It must also have raised the notion that if they accepted this idea, then like all the other murders of the previous decade it would almost certainly remain forever unsolved; something Inspector Swanson must have been desperate to avoid, but something the press was all too eager to highlight.

But it was the early newspaper editions, with their lurid descriptions of the murder, that brought the first breakthrough. At half past six that morning, police had issued a description of the dead woman, which was picked up and published by most local newspapers:

> Found dead with throat cut, a woman, aged twenty-five; height about five feet; hair and eyes light brown; left ear torn with earring; enlargement of third knuckle of right hand; black jet earring, black clothes, and crepe hat; light button boots, striped stockings.

A few lines with little by way of characterisation but which brought a number of women to the doors of Leman Street police station, described by the *Daily Telegraph* as being, 'slatternly, with dishevelled hair, bruised and scarred faces, and a sorry look altogether'. In other words, to use the police assessment of their character, women 'of low class'.

But what these women were able to confirm was that the murder victim had, without doubt, been working in prostitution; that her first name was definitely Frances and that she had been moving around the Whitechapel area and sleeping in various common lodging houses, the last located on Thrawl Street.

Though, as police had learnt from the murders of three years earlier, that was all they were ever likely to learn. Experience had taught them that whilst these women had been acquainted with the victim they were not to be trusted on detail. Surnames were not common currency in Whitechapel and whilst some of these women clearly knew who she was, it would only have been by loose association. They would have known her to speak to in the street or drink with in a pub, but rarely did they ever enquire into each other's background. Life was unpredictable enough and friendships transitory, leaving little time, and even less inclination, to discover more about your neighbour than was necessary to facilitate an untroubled passage through a life rife with poverty and deprivation. Often the familiar saying, 'the less you know the better', fitted their life on the street.

But it was a start, and despite police reservations about what could and could not be given credence when listening to these women, there was also one other skill they possessed which was invaluable: they were observant and why would they not be? Public houses were their meeting places. They could find their way around Whitechapel simply guided by the names above the pub doors. It was where they touted for business. Business they then took on to the streets late at night. It also meant they saw or talked to lots of individuals sharing the same spaces and often what they saw, or heard, was passed around between them. By late morning, the stories of what some had seen the previous night began to surface and police paid attention.

When Chief Inspector Donald Swanson called together his officers for a second meeting just after lunch it was to discuss, in part, one particular story which had begun to surface and one he considered most credible. The still officially unnamed woman found beneath Arch 45 had spent much of the previous night in the company of a ship's fireman. No name had been given at that stage, no real description either, only that the man had recently come off a ship in London Docks. To any officers who had been involved in the protracted investigations over the Ripper killings, the mention of a connection to the sea rang alarm bells. Speculation had at times raged over the possibility the Whitechapel serial killer had been some sort of sailor, a man who, after he killed, had slipped back into the docks, re-joined his ship and sailed away. It was a plausible theory, fuelled from time to time by various stories published in the media, supporting the notion and suggesting either he had served on a Spanish ship or one of the many cattle boats sailing in and out of London Docks.

The idea could not be ignored and under the direction of Inspector Regan, Thames police mounted a search of all boats moored or about to sail. Thirty-five vessels in total between London and Blackwell were boarded, their crew lists checked, and their holds searched. It took time and the police carrying out the searches were extremely thorough, given their remit, which perhaps was not as comprehensive as it might have been. Their prime concern seems to have been to ensure the right number of men were on any ship searched; that their names matched the crew lists, and there were no stowaways. According to the *Telegraph*, that resulted in nothing tangible being found, which is perhaps unsurprising. It was extremely difficult to get past guards on the dock gates in the early hours of the morning unseen. What was considerably easier was returning to a ship that had your name on the crew list, and perhaps not enough attention was paid to those that had.

Though by the time Inspector Regan reported his findings back to Leman Street police station, things had moved on significantly. The ship's fireman, believed to have been with the murdered woman on the night of her death, had been named as James Sadler, and police were out on the streets trying to find him. Press reports also created a vocal network across Whitechapel which eventually revealed the woman's identity as Frances Coles, local to the area and well-known to a few lodging housekeepers. These details, which had been revealed by the heavier than normal police presence on the streets, had also begun to produce witnesses to her movements during the hours prior to her death.

James Coles, the victim's father, had also been located and brought to the mortuary from the Bermondsey Workhouse where he had been living having been unable to find work. So too had his other daughter, Mary Ann, who lived close by. Both made the formal identification that finally gave a name to the victim. In their later statements, despite what police believed they already knew about Frances and her lifestyle, the family's view of how Frances had been living differed significantly from that of the police. To them, Frances had been a hard-working young woman, employed locally and living a respectable life with a reputable old lady at 32 Richardson Street, off Commercial Road, and also holding down a job at Winfield Hora & Co, a wholesale druggist in the Minories. Whether or not they were simply in denial is debateable. Police by this time had already met with a man claiming to have lived with Frances on and off between 1883 and 1887. He was James Murray, who had been working as a labourer in Bethnal Green and, according to what he had told police, Frances had been working as a prostitute for the previous eight years. She was living at Wilmot's Lodging House on Thrawl Street when he first met her, and he claimed, using the surname of Coleman. Furthermore, he told police, she had been walking the streets around Shoreditch and Bow, as well as Whitechapel. Paid employment was never on the agenda as far as Frances was concerned – leastways not as far as he knew. In turn, that lack of stability, he thought, had led to her becoming more dependent on alcohol. Whenever he had seen her, in recent times or perhaps met her by chance, he claimed he could tell she had 'given way to drunken habits'. Why she had used a false surname, he could not explain. although in his statement to police he seemed to accept it had always been false. Perhaps because he knew her father, James Coles, and had visited him from time to time at the workhouse.

This was a view shared by police, who made a note to the same effect at the end of Murray's statement which both Inspector Moore and Superintendent Arnold endorsed. Essentially, they accepted at that point that Murray's claim of a previous long-standing relationship with the dead woman was credible and that it supported the later formal identification made by the Coles family, therefore removing any further future speculation by the press. Any doubts regarding her chosen occupation were dispelled after officers made a visit to 32 Richardson Street to interview the old lady who had rented her rooms only to find there was no such place. Winfield Hora & Co also confirmed that whilst Frances had at one time been employed by them, that had been eight years earlier and only on a day labour basis, which meant she had no fixed working hours – quite possibly what forced her on to the streets. Insecure working hours meant no wage guarantee, which in turn meant she would have been unable to pay for food, clothing, rent and all the other things necessary to support a safe, more secure life.

Whilst all this information was being gathered by police, Coroner Mr Wynne Baxter had opened the inquest into the murder at the Working Lads' Institute in Whitechapel Road. The hearing was intentionally brief at that stage, purely procedural and not unusual; confirmation of identity had not been communicated to the coroner before the court sat. In many ways it was also perhaps fortuitous. Mr Baxter had only eight of the nominated fourteen jurors in court. Those missing had already sent representatives to explain their absence or act as substitutes, which was frustrating as it delayed proceedings and forced the coroner to select additional jurors from amongst those attending court. Again, this was not unusual; reluctance to sit as a coroner's juror was not unheard of.

Public service or duty, depending upon one's point of view, was not always seen with a virtuous eye as it came at a cost. Jurors were not paid for attendance, something Mr Wynne Baxter was well aware of. Nevertheless, he resolved the issues quickly, took evidence from police regarding the discovery and then adjourned until 17 February.

That gave police a further forty-eight hours to pull together a case file that would not only account for parts of her life but, more importantly, how she had spent the last hours of it. Street enquiries had inevitably begun to reveal some of her movements on the night she died. They had also produced a more accurate description of James Sadler, the sailor they knew she had been seen drinking with prior to her murder. His arrest was obviously top of the list. It was also key to the investigation that they account for Frances's movements in or around Swallow Gardens. Who had seen her in or around the vicinity and just what had brought her to Arch 45?

The questions are obvious enough and the most difficult ones to answer. But the fact she had been working on the streets suggested she would have known the topography of Whitechapel extremely well and would have understood how Swallow Gardens late at night, sometimes favoured her business. Though whether the early hours of a morning were seen as favourable was perhaps debateable. Certainly, she would have known how the archway at its centre offered the kind of short-term privacy her clients were paying for and how it could have given easy, unobserved access, back to the docks. No doubt crucial factors when dealing with men from the ships moored nearby. As to reliable witness sightings of Frances herself, accompanied or alone, anywhere near the murder site, there are none. Despite what we may think today, at two o'clock in the morning in 1891 the streets were generally quiet, particularly on a cold February night.

By midday on Saturday, 14 February there was still much work to do, but there were also some positives. Identity had clearly been established, so had her occupation and a picture was slowly coming together that would, at the very least, fill in some of the gaps around her movements prior to her death. There was also a prime suspect. Obviously, it was too early to be sure but clearly the finger of suspicion had already begun to point in the direction of James Sadler, prematurely or not. Understandable, given that everything known about the man at that early stage indicated he had spent a significant amount of time with Frances on the night of her death. No other suspect had surfaced and there had been an intriguing statement, made by a railway man, which suggested Sadler may have been around Swallow Gardens at the right time.

William 'Jumbo' Friday, the GNR man Kate McCarthy had seen in the early hours of the morning, after reading a newspaper article about the murder, had convinced himself that the couple he had seen in the doorway on Royal Mint Street were the victim and her killer and paid a visit to Leman Street to inform police of his sighting.

According to Superintendent Arnold's report about the events of Friday, 13 February, he was clearly certain the woman he had seen was Frances Coles:

> At 1.45 a.m. he (Friday) was passing through Royal Mint Street on his way to the stables when he saw a man and a woman standing in a doorway. He could not discern their faces distinctly but noticed that the woman wore a black hat. He has seen the hat worn by the deceased and identified it as that worn by the woman he saw talking in Royal Mint Street.

If he was right, then the man with her could well have been James Sadler. Pure conjecture, obviously, but conceivable. To be fair to Thomas Arnold, though, it seems he always had doubts over the relevance of the statement William Friday made; hats were commonplace in 1891 and styles similar. What he really needed was a better description of the couple in the doorway and less of the hat if it were to help move the investigation forward – and that was never forthcoming. Nevertheless, it had to be seen as being, potentially, a corroborating piece of evidence in support of the theory that perhaps she had taken a client to Arch 45, and that the client could well have been the sailor they were looking for.

This was a theory they were able to put to the test later that Saturday afternoon, after news broke that Police Sergeant John Don had apprehended James Sadler in the Phoenix public house, Upper East Smithfield.

Chapter 3

James Thomas Sadler

Chief Inspector Swanson met Sadler as he arrived at Leman Street police station. There had been no difficulty in finding him once his description had been passed around Whitechapel, and Sadler had made no attempt to hide away. According to Sergeant Don, who apprehended him, he had been sitting inside the Phoenix public house expecting to be found and was quite calm. News of Frances Coles's murder had obviously swept across Whitechapel and Sadler was no fool. He knew well enough that he would eventually be named as the man who had spent time with her prior to her murder, but had made the decision to stay put and hope it all went away. Why volunteer to put yourself into the centre of a murder enquiry if it could be avoided? And he liked a drink, so, like the condemned man with nowhere to hide, he kept an eye on the bar room door and just waited.

Local man, Samuel Harris, eventually gave him away. There was no arrest, no scuffle, no argument. The sergeant did as protocol demanded and simply asked him to step outside, explained why he was needed back at Leman Street police station, and marched him away. He had done it before and knew the rules well enough: pay attention, ask no questions but listen and record any conversation, and Sadler was all too prepared to talk. So much so, when Swanson sat down later to interview him, he already knew he was married, had known Frances for some time and on the night of her death had bought her a hat. All freely given information which perhaps suggested Sadler was likely to be reasonably forthcoming when questioned about his life, even if reticent about events surrounding the murder. And so he was, although when it came to the night in question, he was less communicative and more forgetful. Alcohol, he claimed, had dulled his senses, and clouded his memory, an assertion Swanson had to accept at face value, though probably with some scepticism. This was borne out to some extent in the statement Sadler made, which was long and rambling (see Appendix 1) though in the main largely factual and, on the face of it, not too difficult to verify. Like any modern-day police force, of course, H Division would begin their enquiries to assess its veracity within hours of it being made. Some facts being more easily checked than others, as is often the case.

He explained how he had arrived in Whitechapel on 11 February after being discharged from the steamship SS *Fez*, where he had worked as a ship's fireman, at around seven o'clock at night. After paying a visit to the Victoria for the first drink of the night, he had walked to the pub opposite, the Princess Alice, and had met Frances Coles at some time between 8.30 and 9 p.m. He said he had known Frances for eighteen months.

On an earlier occasion the two of them, he claimed, had spent a night together at some lodging house on Thrawl Street. That would have been in the summer of 1889, though the exact dates he could not remember. But clearly, she had made an impression. So much so that when he saw her a second time in the same pub it had seemed reasonable to assume they could pick up from where they left off and spend another night together. After all, he had money in his pocket and no doubt Frances was happy to help him spend it – something she apparently acknowledged, according to Sadler, because shortly after meeting she had asked that they leave the Princess Alice before he spent too much of it. Too many people in the bar, she told him, would have expected some of that money to be spent on them. So, apparently, without too much persuasion, he had agreed, and together they made the short walk to a pub on the corner of Dorset Street, which he couldn't name, but it was where they met a woman named Annie Lawrence in the bar; not someone he had ever met before but a friend to Frances. The night eventually ended when Frances agreed she would stay with him all night if he paid for a bed at a nearby lodging house in White's Row. He could not remember what time of night that was but did recall he had bought a half bottle of whisky to take away with them. That saw them through what was left of the night, and they did not leave until sometime between 11 a.m. and noon the next day.

His memory of that following day, the 12 February, was vague. From his statement, it appears the pair of them drank their way through much of it, so it is perhaps not too surprising. What he did recall was it involved visiting a number of pubs, the names of which, in most cases, escaped him. Although there were one or two he did remember:

> [O]ne of which was the Bell, Middlesex Street. We stayed for about two hours drinking and laughing. When in the Bell she [Frances] spoke to me about a hat which she had paid a shilling off a month previously. We then went on the way to the bonnet shop drinking at the pub houses on the way … I gave her the half a crown, which was due for the hat, and she went into the shop. She came out again and said that her hat was not ready the woman is putting some elastic on. We then went into a public house in White's or Bakers Row and we had more drinks then she went for her hat, and got it and brought it to me at the pub.

Swanson knew the hat to be significant; Sadler rambled on and told him that he had asked Frances to throw the old hat away, but she had refused. Instead, she pinned it on to her dress because she wanted to keep it. From there, he said, the two of them walked to Brick Lane where they paid a visit to the Marlborough Head pub and carried on drinking. He stayed there with Frances until he remembered he had arranged to meet a man named Nichols in Spittal Street. He claimed to have made the appointment alone, he and Frances meeting up again later – exactly where he could not remember – but he did recall that when they met again, she had told him she wanted to go back to some lodging house near Thrawl Street:

> We came down Thrawl Street and while going down a woman
> with a red shawl struck me on the head and I fell down and
> when down I was kicked by some men around me ... I found
> my money and my watch gone. I was then penniless, and
> I then had a row with Frances for I thought she might have
> helped me when I was down. I then left her at the corner of
> Thrawl Street without making any appointment.

Sadler went on to say he made his way to the docks after the robbery and tried to return to the SS *Fez*. He never got to the ship. He was stopped by a police sergeant and a constable who blocked the dock gates and refused him entry. Unfortunately, he had no idea of the time. What he did remember was that after being stopped, and because by his own testimony he was drunk, he managed to get himself into an argument with a number of dock labourers. That then led to a fight in which he sustained a cut to his head and severe bruising to his ribs and as a result of the beating he needed to take some time out. 'I then turned down Nightingale Lane and the labourers went up Smithfield way. I remained in Nightingale Lane for about a quarter of an hour feeling my injuries.'

Again, he had no idea of time. But from there, obviously badly bruised, sore, and still apparently bleeding from the head, he made his way to the Victoria Lodging House in East Smithfield in the hope that he could get a bed for the night. But he was out of luck. With no money after the mugging, the house refused to let him stay so he went walkabout, for how long he again said he had no idea. However, he did remember that at some point in the night, he had returned to the same lodging house he and Frances had stayed at the night before in the hope that she would still be there. She was, but not in any fit state to hold a conversation. He told Swanson he had found her in the lodging house's kitchen slumped over a table with her head resting on her arms, sleeping:

> I spoke to Frances about her hat. She appeared half dazed from drink and I asked her if she had enough money to pay the double bed with. She said she had no money, and I told (her) I had not a farthing but I had four pounds 15/- coming to me ... I then went to the deputy and asked for a night's lodgings on the strength of the money I was to lift next day ... I was eventually turned out by a man and left Frances behind at the house.

From there he claimed to have made his way to the London hospital and remembered being stopped on Whitechapel Road by a young policeman who checked him over because, as he apparently told him, he appeared to be in a bad way. Subsequently, he managed to reach the hospital where they let him stay until about eight o'clock in the morning, when he left. He attempted to get back into the Victoria Lodging House but was again turned away so returned to the docks where he eventually collected the money outstanding to him.

Swanson pressed him to try and establish some sort of timeline. But Sadler remained stubbornly vague though he did eventually remember roughly how late in the day it had been when he was attacked and robbed: 'As far as I can think it was between five and six that I was assaulted in Thrawl Street; at any rate it was getting dark, and it was some hours after that that I went to the London Docks.'

Far too vague a testimony to rule him out and not enough to rule him in, it left Swanson in a quandary. Sadler, it would seem in his opinion at that time, still had to be the main suspect. Swanson's probable thinking at that juncture was along the lines of a man trying to be deliberately vague in order not to incriminate himself. Clearly, for police at the end of that interview, the inevitable follow-up enquiries had to be diligent, thorough and comprehensive if they were to establish a credible timeline. If James Sadler was their killer, then it was not illogical to believe the man was also the Ripper; there is enough evidence to suggest that Swanson was not ruling it out. At the end of the interview, with that thought clearly in mind, he asked Sadler to provide him with a list of the ships he had sailed on over the last few years:

> My last discharges are as follows – last – discharge 11.2.90 in London ship Fez – next discharge 6.9.90 London, next discharge 15.7.90 London, next discharge 27.5.90 Barry, next discharge 1.10.89 London, next 2.10.88 London. Engaged 17.8.88, next 5.5 87 engaged. 24.3.87 London.

Swanson obviously needed to know if he could put Sadler into Whitechapel on all the relevant dates of the 1888 killing spree. But like the rest of James Sadler's statement, it was vague; the lack of clarity a problem to the chief inspector but not impossible to verify. He would have known how the London docks worked and how every ship had to have a crew list which showed the date of sailing, destination, salary paid, name of sailor, date he joined, and date he left. This information would be invaluable and key to confirming the scant information Sadler had given him. So, to that end, he had Inspector Moore and Superintendent Arnold organise a complete and in-depth investigation of Sadler's seagoing life and add, where they could, pub names and appropriate times to Sadler's statement. The latter was crucial if he were to place Frances and the sailor together, as Sadler had claimed they were, and maybe even create some sort of timeline around the scant detail that would either corroborate or invalidate.

Swanson also decided he wanted to know where Sadler's wife was. What was the relationship between the two of them? Where had they been living, particularly three years ago? In the statement the only reference Sadler made to her was at the very end: 'My wife resides in the country, but I would prefer not to mention it.'

There was no more. Yet he had volunteered information to Sergeant Don that implied the two of them were still living together. How true was that? How married, in fact, was he?

Clearly those multiple murders of three years earlier were being considered alongside the murder of Frances Coles. Absolutely sensible. If they had stumbled across the Whitechapel killer beneath Arch 45, as a number of his officers believed, then either Swanson had to prove it or show no clear link. Sadler, by his own admission, was a sailor, a man familiar with the docks and the ships, but his statement also showed a knowledge of the streets around Whitechapel and that made him a credible suspect, not just in the case of Frances Coles or Alice McKenzie in the summer of 1889 but also all the other unsolved murders from that decade. Quite rightly, Inspector Swanson wanted, and needed, to be thorough.

Chapter 4

Frances Coles

Whilst enquiries into James Sadler's movements continued, police were also building a profile, of sorts, to fit Frances Coles. Information was scant and it is doubtful they were too concerned with her past. Her status within Whitechapel was, by this time, reasonably well established. Additional information was garnered from her father, James, and sister Mary Ann who had made that formal identification; none of it was particularly informative, neither of them being aware of the lifestyle Frances had followed in the years prior to her death. Perhaps this is difficult to imagine, particularly between the sisters, but absolutely nothing to suggest otherwise has ever emerged. As far as they were concerned, Frances had been in continual employment since moving away from home. Not that Frances appears to have ever known a stable home life.

James, who had been born in Somerset, always declared himself to be a shoemaker whenever he completed a census, but it would appear work had rarely been regular and never permanent. Whether that was due to an injury he had sustained to his leg or whether it had been down to the vagaries of the shoe industry is now impossible to know. But certainly, times throughout his life had been hard and money often scarce, which is perhaps why police found him living in the Bermondsey workhouse at the age of 70 and not for the first time either. He, along with 14-year-old Frances and her brother, had found themselves there for the first time in 1873. So, it is not difficult to understand how life for Frances, given that experience and the abject poverty she would have seen all around her, offered little hope of future prosperity. The East End of London, made up of tenements and lodging houses, where street thefts, rows, fights and drunks were commonplace, was a poor advert for the capital. Lighting was poor, street cleaning non-existent and housing, what there was of it, was in the hands of unscrupulous landlords and of poor quality. The area's close proximity to the docks and the sailors that sought out its pubs were a source of hidden wealth for the various local businesses and an almost subsidised access to prostitution.

This then was Frances Coles's world: familiar in every aspect and unrewarding in most. A difficult, arduous environment in which to make any sort of viable financial impact, particularly as a single woman living outside the family home with rooms to find, along with rent and food to pay for. Though just how or why her family home had broken up is difficult to discover. She had been born into a family of five: two sisters, Selina and Mary Ann; a brother James; her father; and her mother, Mary, who according to the 1871 census had been born in Scotland not Ireland as is often reported. Doubt has always existed over whether her parents ever married. James had declared himself single whilst living at the workhouse in 1891 but not on the 1871 census return. There, her mother Mary, who was 40 at the time, had put herself down as being his wife and she shared his surname. So, who knows? They would not have been the first to lie about their marital status.

Certainly, James Murray, who had given the statement to police about he and Frances being together for around four years in the mid-1880s (1883–7) would have known more about her and her family's past lifestyle but was never asked by police. Neither did he ever volunteer more information in that regard, even though, by his own admission, he visited her father on several occasions at the Bermondsey Workhouse and must have been familiar with how all the family relationships worked. Neither did he correct James Coles in his belief that his daughter had a stable working life when he knew, as he had told police, in all the time he had known her she had never held down a job. That – the employed side of Frances

Coles's life – had all happened long before he had arrived on the scene. As he indicated during his police interview, if there had ever been a paid job it had been long before he ever met her. But what we know today is that up until about 1882/3 she had worked for two different employers. At around 17 years of age (in 1877) she had been employed by James Sinclair & Son, 65 Southwark Street who are described in business journals as manufacturing soap and other toiletries. Whilst there, she changed her name to Frances Coleman and started working life as a trainee in their packing department. That lasted for around five years. By 1881, she was living around Whitechapel, still using the name Coleman, and walking to the Minories every day to work for Winfield Hora & Co., a wholesale druggist trading mainly in the export trade. Her job, which has been widely publicised over the years, was in the bottling plant. There she put the stoppers into bottles or stuck on labels. Mundane work no doubt and also problematic. Securing stoppers into bottles was not as easy as perhaps it would appear to our eyes today. Automation was something that belonged to the future, which meant the impact of such repetitive work on the fingers was severe. Stoppers had to be twisted into place, which over time caused calluses to form on the knuckles, something Frances suffered from. The work was also paid on a day labour basis. There were no guaranteed hours; she only worked when they called her in. Whether her job had started out that way is not now known but is highly likely and maybe for Frances this kind of loose arrangement worked. Certainly, as far as is known, she made no attempt to find work elsewhere, though the money she earned would have been at the poorer end of the scale. Judged on what we know of women's income in other similar industries it would have amounted to no more than around a shilling a day. Tough when you have to keep a roof over your head. But Hora's appears to have been her only legitimate source of income at that time and she stayed with them for around three years. Perhaps that is where the prostitution began. A supplementary source of income, a sort of fill-in when the hours and the pay were low. Then at some point in 1883 she decided there was more money on the street than in the factory. This is completely understandable to some extent but, nevertheless, a decision that rendered her extremely vulnerable as things eventually turned out. Poor daily rates and what we would term zero-hours contracts were commonplace in Victorian England. It is disappointing when you see how much some of these London-based industries were earning and Winfield Hora was no exception. The company was hugely successful and had created a worldwide market. So much so, when Henry Winfield died in 1904 at the age of 75, he left behind an estate valued at £20,979 (equal to around £1.8 million today).

Day labour was clearly good for company profits but not for the individual and, in Frances's case, even if the hours had been more regular, perhaps not as lucrative as prostitution. Frances was 23 years old or thereabouts when she gave up on paid work; pretty, slim, and very likely well versed in how the street prostitutes around her worked. Easy, perhaps, to fit in amongst women she no doubt knew, drank with occasionally or shared living space with. She would also have known how vice in the East End functioned, the clientele, the public houses they frequented and how the women funded their lifestyle. So, to her at least, the decision to go on the streets would have held some merit. Society seemed to hold conflicting views. According to *Sir Howard Vincent's Police Code 1889* prostitution was not necessarily illegal: 'Prostitutes cannot legally be taken into custody simply because they are prostitutes; to justify their apprehension they must commit some distinct act which is an offence against the law.'

Essentially, that meant any prosecution of a prostitute resulting in a case being brought to court required someone to first complain and then that same person appear at a police court to give accusatory evidence. This, for obvious reasons, was a highly unlikely event when these same courts were the constant haunt of newspaper reporters. So, prostitution had a few advantages, though it is fair to say there were also a few unavoidable vices, disease and alcohol being at the top of the list. As far as is known, Frances had never suffered from the former but definitely had a taste for the latter. Even her sister Mary Ann had noticed her penchant for drink. So had the local police who knew Frances by sight, if not so much by name, because she had been a regular on Whitechapel's streets late at night intoxicated. Public houses, it seems, were where most of her clients came from; men from the docks, both labourers and seamen, as James Sadler had attested to, were drawn to them. Why not? This was Victorian England, a strait-laced society dominated by the Church and its teachings, where sexual repression was the accepted norm. But where, hidden amongst the streets and public houses of Whitechapel, sex was a currency to be bought and sold to those that had the money to pay and dockworkers and sailors did just that and, as history has shown, they were not the only ones either.

Frances began to move around this seedy side of London life. She also began to move around the various lodging houses scattered across the district, and there were hundreds of them. Thrawl Street, George Street, Dorset Street, Commercial Street, Flower and Dean Street, to name but a few, housed a number of cheap, inferior quality lodging houses. Here you could get a bed for the night for 4d, but there were rules.

Lodging houses were defined as being either gender specific or available to both sexes. For Frances she would have generally made use of the latter, described, according to the police code 1889, as a 'common lodging house', and defined as being: 'one in which persons of the poorer classes are received for short periods, and, though promiscuously brought together, are allowed to inhabit one common room'.

They had to be licensed and were legally required to display a placard stating the number of beds for which that licence was held. The bed linen had to be changed on a weekly basis, the windows had to be opened at 10 a.m. every day to allow ventilation and there had to be a common kitchen where those staying could cook whatever they wished. Generally, these places were owned by landlords who lived far enough away from the premises to be unaware of what took place within them. To ensure the premises operated as the law demanded, the owners would employ a warden or keeper whose name and address had to be registered with the local authority. They were normally to be found seated behind a small window, just beyond the outside entrance door into the building. Their job was to take the money from those wanting a bed and essentially manage the upkeep of the house. The average cost of a bed was essentially fixed at 4d a night. For those that could afford to go a little up market there were furnished lodgings. These usually consisted of a bed, two chairs and maybe a table. Average cost here was about 8d per night.

Although not the most hygienic places to stay, they were certainly the most cost effective for those that had little money. They obviously suited Frances Coles because she made use of them throughout the late 1880s right up until her death, which is not too surprising when you consider the variable income she would have earned as a prostitute. It also explains how and why she would have been known to the men in blue. The police's H Division, centred around Leman Street police station, contained within its boundary, which was the Whitechapel district west and east of Commercial Street, some 233 houses and sixty-two known brothels, according to a Home Office Report of 1888/9. All of which made it almost impossible for a woman operating as Frances had done to keep a low profile, particularly after the Ripper murders of 1888 when numbers of police on foot patrol increased significantly.

For those who could not afford the few coppers it cost for a bed, there was only the workhouse, somewhere Frances Coles would have been keen to avoid, being all too familiar with the appalling regimented way in which workhouses were run. If James Sadler's statement is to be believed it also explains why both of them ended up in the kitchen of the lodging house in White's Row. No money, no bed.

This is a scenario Donald Swanson would have well understood, having spent some years at the sharp end of policing in Whitechapel. It went some way to explaining just why Frances had been back out on the street in the early hours of the morning and perhaps why it made her so vulnerable. What he now needed to know was just how had her injuries been inflicted, and could they have been caused by the infamous Whitechapel murderer, or could it have been Sadler the sailor? And if it was, had they just caught Jack the Ripper?

PART TWO

INVESTIGATION

Chapter 5

Timelines

The answer to that question was still some way off, but with James Sadler's statement on their desk, police now had something to work with. By his own admission, he had spent a significant amount of time with Frances over two days. Although his statement was vague, it gave them an outline, of sorts, of the events that had taken place between the two of them and a reasonable idea as to where they had spent most of their time. But it was no confession. What it gave the investigating officers was the start of a timeline. All they had to do was fill in the blanks, something they spent much of 15 February trying to do and they were reasonably successful. So much so, that after spending forty hours in custody at Leman Street police station James Sadler was formally charged with murder at midnight that same day by Detective Inspector Moore. He then searched Sadler and found a purse containing £2 17s 4d, eight lottery tickets, a quantity of loose tobacco, a postal order for £2 and a number of seaman's discharge papers, but nothing of an incriminating nature. Moore's reasoning for making that formal charge, officially stated as a charge of 'wilfully causing the death of Frances Coles', is not too difficult to fathom. As part of the investigation into the events surrounding the murder and the hours that had followed it, detective sergeants Record and Ward had interviewed a man named Duncan Campbell, a fellow sailor staying at the Sailors' Home in Well Street, Whitechapel. He had turned up at Leman Street police station two days after the murder claiming Sadler had walked into the Sailors' Home at around 10.15 a.m. on 13 February, some eight hours after the discovery of Frances Coles's body beneath Arch 45 and offered to sell him a knife. According to a report in the *West Cumberland Mail*, which picked up the story several days later, they described that knife as being 'peculiarly shaped', and bought by Campbell for a shilling, unaware at the time that there had been a murder committed in Swallow Gardens. On the following day, Saturday, short of money himself, he had washed it and sold it on, only learning of Frances Coles's murder on the Sunday morning – which is what had prompted him to go to the Leman Street police station and report the incident.

Within hours of that statement being made, police had located the second buyer and recovered the knife. Sadler was then placed in a hastily set up identity parade and picked out by Campbell – confirmation as far as Inspector Moore was concerned that they had solved the case. It was enough, they had the murder weapon and the man that had owned it at the time of the murder. How could it not be? The logic was sound. The facts, loose though they were, were irrefutable and finding the knife an unexpected bonus. It had to be James Sadler ... didn't it?

Obviously, James Sadler, being held at this time at the Arbour Square police station, felt very differently but had no idea at that stage of coming proceedings or exactly what the evidence was that had put him in the cells. First indications of the credibility of that evidence came on the following day, when he appeared before the Thames police court, on the afternoon of 16 February, before magistrate Mr Mead where he gave his address as being the Victoria Lodging House, Upper East Smithfield. In attendance were Superintendent Thomas Arnold and Chief Inspector Swanson. The inspector as an observer, the superintendent to request that *only* evidence of the arrest be heard. Obviously, they felt at this early stage of proceedings they needed more time to build their case, but the court refused.

Mead argued that it was inappropriate to do so without some evidence in support of the charge being heard. He was right. There were no legal advocates present in that court, which meant no cross-examination or legal argument would have been possible. All Mead was interested in was the veracity of the evidence that had led police to make the charge in the first place. Sadler himself had no representation but was allowed to challenge where appropriate. The court's only purpose, as Mead well knew, was to decide if the evidence collected was germane to the charge levied. In turn, that meant both defendant and the public at large had the right to hear the case for murder presented in a court, for the first time.

Although just what evidence could be presented, Mead would have known well enough was likely to be scant and incomplete. He was an experienced magistrate, and this he would have known was essentially only the first round in what could eventually become a long, protracted criminal trial. But that would be weeks ahead – if it got that far. At this stage, he intended the hearing to be brief; an evidential summary of what police had in relation to Sadler that would keep him in a prison cell.

The hearing opened with evidence from the man who had helped police find Sadler, Samuel Harris, who, it turned out, had also been a fellow lodger at the house in White's Row, used by both Sadler and Frances Coles, and who was able to corroborate Sadler's police statement about both of them being in the kitchen of that lodging house on the night she died:

> I had been there about an hour and a half when I saw a woman
> I knew by the name of Frances. She was sitting on a form,
> with her head resting on the table. That was in the kitchen of
> the lodging house. About half past eleven I saw a man come
> in. The prisoner is that man.

He went on to tell the court that Sadler had tried to talk with Frances, who apparently showed no interest, insisting that he had been robbed. According to Harris, very little conversation took place between the two of them and at around half past midnight Sadler had left, alone.

Sergeant Westley-Edwards, H Division, added to that testimony when he told the court that at around 2 a.m. Sadler was on Tower Hill, looking somewhat battered about the face and bleeding. When stopped and questioned he had claimed to have been fighting down on the docks, which he had said explained his injuries. The sergeant told the court that as a result of that explanation he had examined Sadler to check he was not seriously hurt and had then watched him walk off in the general direction of the Minories.

That was followed by testimony from hospital night porter William Fewell, who told the court Sadler had turned up at the hospital about three hours later, around 5 a.m., had been treated for his injuries and eventually sent out again at about half past six in the morning.

Three pieces of testimony, in no way damning but intended to show that Sadler had been on the streets between midnight and 2 a.m. If Westley-Edwards was correct in his time keeping and Sadler's direction of travel was towards the Minories, then he was in the vicinity of Swallow Gardens at the right time – Swallow Gardens and its archway passage towards Chamber Street being only minutes away on foot from where he had last been seen. Speculation of course, but probably enough of a hypothesis to warrant holding Sadler as a suspect, if nothing else.

Mr Mead agreed and after hearing testimony as to time and place with regard to the discovery of Frances Coles's body and its location inside Archway 45 he invited James Sadler to ask any relevant questions should he wish to. He declined, citing lack of food and general ill health as being prohibitive to his ability to do himself justice, which was enough for Mr Mead to then remand him back into police custody.

It seems clear that at that juncture, even without testimony about the discovery of the knife, which was still being examined, that as far as the police court was concerned enough evidence existed to hold Sadler on suspicion. Though Mr Mead, experienced as he was, would also have known everything he had been presented with was circumstantial at best; more would be needed to affect any conviction for murder. No doubt for Sadler, who at that stage had possibly still not been made aware of why Duncan Campbell had picked him out from a line-up, it was disappointing if not unexpected. Nothing of note had been heard in that courtroom and certainly nothing seriously incriminating. Did he realise there was more to come? If so, he would have been right.

The resumed inquest opened before Coroner Mr Wynne Baxter the next day, 17 February, again at the Working Lads' Institute, Whitechapel. With the victim's identity now confirmed he took character evidence from Frances Coles's father, James, and her sister Mary Ann, both of whom continued to insist they knew nothing of her involvement in street prostitution. Neither seemed aware of her true age either. James Coles insisted she was 26 years old and as far as can be ascertained, her sister Mary Ann never contested this. But Frances Coles was actually 31 (born 1859). It seems reasonable, therefore, to accept that if they had no idea of when she had been born, they also had no idea what she had been doing to earn money either. It is probably fair to say they were not a close family and given the circumstances of the life they had been living over the previous twenty years, it is understandable as to why. Life in the East End of London at this time was hard for a family struggling to make ends meet, and incredibly stressful. From what little we know about James Coles, unemployment had been a regular visitor and moving home a common occurrence, which would have made future prospects for all of them bleak. Little wonder that Frances tried to hide her fall into penury and prostitution. Not that any of that mattered to the coroner's court. All that concerned Mr Baxter's court were the circumstances of her death. It was for others to care about the social deprivations suffered by many of the victims that caused his court to sit. But for the police it was the first step towards bringing James Sadler to trial for murder. For them, all that mattered was that the coroner's jury hear all the evidence and pronounce against him.

To that end, their investigations into Sadler's movements whilst he had been held at Arbour Square police station had been thorough and the assembled evidence was leaning towards his guilt, with no interest in trying to prove his innocence. From the minute they had taken him from the Phoenix public house, it is clear the police believed him guilty and, as far as can be deduced today from police files, there were no other suspects. When the inquest opened, police genuinely believed they had their man and perhaps also the Ripper. Certainly, press speculation followed the same line. They pursued the story with a vigour not seen since 1888. The spectre that haunted Whitechapel's streets three years earlier was resurrected and the prisoner in the dock judged guilty before he even arrived in court. Fortunately, Wynne Baxter was not swayed either by police belief or press speculation. He fully understood the protocol to be followed here, as did Superintendent Arnold who again attended along with a representative from the office of the public prosecutor, Charles Mathews. Sadler, as before, had no representation, meaning he was at a great disadvantage. Being under arrest at the time of this second sitting meant that this was a court essentially set up to hear evidence in support of the case against him. Mathews was to play an integral part in proceedings; as a representative of the police his task was to cross-examine where he could, along with the coroner. But both had different aims: the coroner to hear how Frances Coles had met her death; the prosecutor to ascertain whether the evidence presented would aid police in what he believed would become a murder trial. To that end, this was never going to be a long session.

After hearing evidence from Frances Coles's immediate family, it was down to a small number of witnesses whose testimonies were to help pinpoint Sadler's movements on the night she was killed. All, with one exception, were centred on his involvement with Frances at the lodging house in White's Row, the place where they spent the night together on 11 February and where they had returned a day later.

Charles Guiver, night watchman, who had lived at the house for four years, told the court that for three of those years Frances had been a regular visitor: 'She was a casual lodger, staying a night at a time, and sometimes twice a week. She used to bring different men to the lodging house to sleep with her.'

He recalled the last time he had seen her alive was in the kitchen of the lodging house on 12 February at around ten o'clock at night. She had been drunk. Sadler, he told the coroner, had followed her in a little time later. Frances had arrived with two hats. Whether because she was drunk or decided it was no longer needed, he was not sure, but she had thrown one of them on to the fire. Someone else in the room had stepped in to retrieve it before it burnt. He could not recall if Sadler saw that incident, or if Frances took the hat back, but he did remember Sadler's story of his having been robbed and having no money: 'Sadler told me he had been robbed in Thrawl Street of 3s 6d. His face was bleeding, and I advised him to go out into the yard and wash the blood off. I went into the yard with him and helped him bathe the blood away.'

Sadler was not the easiest man to be around either, Guiver recalled. He was belligerent and argumentative, particularly with others in the kitchen. As night watchman, trouble needed to be avoided, so he had tried to get him to go to bed. But, of course, Sadler had no money to pay for lodgings: 'He said he had given Frances a shilling to pay for the bed. The deputy said she hadn't.'

That resulted in another argument, which forced the night watchman to throw him out on to the street: 'It was just before twelve that I turned him out.'

At that point, the coroner wanted to know how he could be so sure of the time and how long after that Frances had followed: 'There is a clock in the office.'

From it he was also sure that Frances had stayed where she was, at that kitchen table until just after 1 a.m.

All of which confirmed a part of Sadler's police statement and helped piece together a part of the timeline he had been vague about. It also helped clear up any confusion over why Frances had been found with two hats. Testimony from the bonnet shop owner Sadler had mentioned also helped place the hat-buying event in place and time.

Peter Lorenzo Hawkes worked with his mother, a milliner, who ran a shop on Nottingham Street, Bethnal Green. According to his testimony, Frances had entered the shop on the night of her murder at between seven and eight o'clock in the evening. Her identity he confirmed after viewing the body at the mortuary. She was, he said, 'three sheets in the wind', meaning well intoxicated, and asked to look at several hats. To him, at that time, she was a stranger, she was poorly dressed and with a man, whom she left standing in the road outside. In contradiction of Sadler's statement, Hawkes made no mention of there being any hat set aside for her nor that had she been paying 1 shilling a month towards its purchase. Simply that after several minutes she picked out a hat she liked and asked for a price. The cost was 1s 11½d:

> After I told her the price she went outside the shop. She went away in the company of a man, who was looking in the left-hand corner of the window. She returned in about two minutes … She gave me 2s, and I gave her a halfpenny change, and she put the hat in a bag. She was wearing a hat at the time. It was a black crepe hat. It was the same pattern as the one I sold with the exception that the one she was wearing had had an edging of beads.

The crucial point of this testimony was not so much the business of buying the hat, important as that was, but about the time, a fact missing from Sadler's statement. Peter Lorenzo recalling the shop visit as being between 7 p.m. and 8 p.m. and Charles Guiver being certain Frances was in the lodging house kitchen until 1 a.m. meant these were two crucial bits of evidence. Pieces of a complex jigsaw that helped to place the Thrawl Street mugging at around 9.30 p.m. The timeline was coming together, but not necessarily in the way police had hoped it would.

This was a factor not lost on Charles Mathews who suddenly realised he and those involved in the police investigation needed more time to reflect: 'Well, gentlemen the evidence is a little contradictory, and I think it will be as well if we have a little time to consider it and sift it. I propose therefore that we now adjourn.'

Coroner Wynne Baxter agreed. Quite what was going through the prosecutor's mind at that point is obviously not known, but it is probable, from the brief testimony he had heard, that whilst the hat-buying incident helped fix the time of the Thrawl Street robbery, Guiver's evidence was detrimental to the police case in that it showed James Sadler and Frances Coles were not together when she left at 1 a.m.

Chapter 6

Doubts

The following day, James Sadler, by now remanded to Holloway Prison, made a decision that probably saved his life. He wrote to the Seamen's Union, an organisation he had joined back in September 1889 when he enrolled as a member of the Burntisland branch. Why, he never explained, but at that time he had been working as a fireman aboard the steamship *SS Loch Latrine*. The ship's Dundee owners were obviously familiar with Burntisland, which is on the northern shore of the Firth of Forth in Fife, and perhaps docked there on occasion. Either way, someone back then had no doubt advised him of the value of membership. It was about to pay dividends:

> Mr Wildgoose from T. Sadler, a stoker, and a member of your union, Burntisland Branch, no 311 (my last payment was made at Tower Hill last Friday, 13th.) … I must apply to you to act as my friend, as I have no claim on anyone else in particular. My wife was always a doubtful friend, my mother is too old, and I have no brother or sister or public house pals worth a damn. I should like a reporter connected with seafaring to watch over me.

The letter went on to express concerns over how the police were conducting their investigations into the Frances Coles murder, questioning their ability to remain impartial and objective in their dealings with himself. He also raised the prospect of their enquiries being biased and expressed a belief they would suppress any evidence in support of his own innocence. What he needed was a courtroom advocate to aid his defence.

Mr Wildgoose readily agreed. Clearly press reportage by this stage was far from impartial, much of which he is likely to have read. Therefore, it is likely that he shared some of James Sadler's concerns. He decided to engage solicitors Wilson and Wallis of Bow Street to begin help mount a defence. They in turn brought in a London barrister, H. H. Lawless to attend the resumption of the inquest and appear at the following police court hearing.

Manna from heaven as far as Sadler was concerned and a key turning point in his defence. Up to this point in proceedings, the police case against him had not proven insurmountable. So far, they had failed to produce any conclusive evidence that showed he was anywhere near the murder site. But, as he well knew, the timeline was still being pieced together, witnesses were still being questioned and his own failure to recall the events of that night was a major problem. Clarity is what was needed and perhaps, in his mind, that was more likely to come from witnesses attending the scheduled coroner's hearing than from himself. The amount of alcohol he had consumed during the day and night of the murder seemed to have rendered him incapable of remembering anything of significance. It is one thing to say you did not do it, it is another thing to prove it. Particularly when the press was still hinting at this being another Ripper murder, which meant a potential future jury possibly influenced by editorial comment. None of which was likely to be favourable.

Sadler was not helped either by the fact that Sarah Sadler, James's estranged wife, had already given an interview to the newspapers which was being used to discredit him. Police were aware and already in the process of trying to find where she was living. James had not been particularly forthcoming in interviews with police about the state of his marriage, initially allowing them to believe the relationship was still strong. But enquiries had already proven that not to be the case and word on the street was they had lived apart for a number of years. Chief Inspector Swanson wanted to know more and had the search widened to find Sarah.

She was found living at 3 Skinner Street, Chatham, some 30-odd miles away from Whitechapel. Swanson, after meeting with Chatham's Superintendent Coppinger, interviewed her on 19 February. It was a difficult meeting. Sarah Sadler had no desire to be dragged into the murder case her husband was involved with, but Swanson proved obdurate and perhaps a little too persuasive. According to his later account of that meeting, he spent his first hour with her trying to overcome her reluctance to take part in any meaningful discussions at all. She insisted she had already said all she was ever going to say about her husband to the newspapers. He argued he had a right to ask about their marriage. A compromise was reached: 'I got from her by question and answer a history of Sadler's employment in London during the time she resided with him.'

This interview was probably crucial, not because she knew anything about the Frances Coles case but because Swanson had to remove James Sadler from his list of Ripper suspects. At the time of this interview, he was still at the top of that list. Just who was James Sadler and where had he been in 1888? All Swanson knew with certainty when he sat down with Sarah Sadler was that James had never come to the attention of Chatham police. Superintendent Coppinger had already carried out his own investigations before Donald Swanson arrived and confirmed that James Sadler had never lived there nor been employed by any Chatham business. Chatham was his wife's home, the place where she had married him and where her mother had lived for years. So Swanson already had a degree of knowledge before he managed to cajole Mrs Sadler into talking to him.

But Swanson was astute enough to realise that if Sadler had been using Chatham as a place to hide no local enquiry would ever have uncovered the fact. That secret would have stayed within his family and the only way of unlocking it was through his wife. So began a long afternoon of probing, penetrating questions, most of which, despite her initial reluctance, Sarah Sadler answered. Though not without rancour at times, and sometimes with a degree of ambiguity, she gave enough detail to allow Swanson to construct a picture of Sadler's past and how it fitted into the exhaustive investigations of 1888.

He had been a sailor at the time of his marriage and his only living relative was his mother, a woman Sarah Sadler had not seen for over six years. Whatever the reason behind that she did not explain; it obviously made no impact on her life so had no relevance. After the wedding, he left the sea having decided to find work on land. At some point between 1876 and 1877, he and his new wife had lived near the Elephant and Castle, Southwark, where he was employed as a labourer at a warehouse in Houndsditch. It did not last, and they moved to a house in Bucks Row, Whitechapel, living by neighbours who worked in the Minories as brush makers. Money was scarce. He had taken a job working for a wool merchant but on a casual basis. She had taken employment as a domestic servant. Lack of funds eventually forced another move, and they took lodgings with a woman named Rose Moriarty near Poplar in London's East End. Sadler then found work with the Metropolitan Stage Carriage Company as a tram conductor. Their finances improved but then there was an incident with a knife. That, according to Sadler's wife, was back in 1880. How serious an incident and what exactly had taken place she refused to clarify. Suffice to say, no one was injured and police were not involved. All Swanson could glean from Mrs Sadler was that the knife in question was a simple folding pocket-knife and that it had been removed from the house and taken away by an Irishwoman whose name she could not remember.

Serious or not, the Sadlers moved from Poplar and James took over the running of a greengrocer's shop in lower Kensington. The business eventually failed. They moved again – this time to Walworth where he went back to labouring in a tea warehouse on Cutter Street, Houndsditch. Later enquiries made by Whitechapel police showed he had remained at that warehouse from December 1881 until July 1888. During the same period, they had lived at two addresses:

Colebrooke Terrace, Bethnal Green, where they lived with a Miss Duffield in 1881, and Johnson Street off Commercial Road in 1888.

In August of that same year, they separated – which must have proved hard for Sarah. There were three daughters, two still living at home, and little money once he left. There was, according to Sarah's story, no reason for him to have left either, especially without explanation, which was why she remained in the house for two weeks waiting for him to return. When he did not come back, she moved back to her mother's at Chatham. There can be little doubt this was the key period Swanson was really interested in, the summer of 1888. Martha Tabram had been murdered on 6 August and Mary Ann Nichols 31 August. Possibly the first two victims, depending upon your point of view, of the Jack the Ripper murder spree. If Sadler had stayed in the area, he stayed on the suspect list. It made sense. By this stage of the Ripper enquiries, the police had explored numerous theories with regard to how the killer had moved around Whitechapel. The press had aired theories of their own and hundreds of column inches had been given over to the debate as to the killer's identity. One hypothesis common to all was that the Whitechapel killer not only knew his way around the place but possibly lived within its boundaries, hence the interest in where Sadler had been living in this time frame. But, frustratingly for Swanson, this was Sarah Sadler's first real blank spot. When her husband had left her that August, he also cut off all communication and it stayed that way between the two of them until March 1889. Then an unexpected letter had apparently arrived at her mother's house in Chatham from Sadler asking Sarah to travel into London and meet him at Fenchurch railway station. Curiosity, she told the inspector, got the better of her so she went along. They had coffee, wandered around the streets, and then spent the night together. He told her he had a job at St Katherine Docks and wanted her to stay a second day. She agreed, perhaps because there was little financial choice. Sadler had apparently made little attempt to make regular maintenance payments, which had forced her to become a mangler taking in washing to earn money. Then they argued again, and she gave up on the idea and returned to Chatham. According to her story, that was the last time they had tried to reconcile but he had visited her in Chatham on occasion over the previous year. Sometimes he would stay one night and on odd occasions he had stayed a week. She offered no dates.

'This was all I was able to get from her after over 2 hours,' wrote Chief Inspector Swanson in his report detailing the meeting. But he wanted to know more. There were gaps in the timeline, some detail was vague, others needed further explanation. So, as soon as he arrived back in London, he had officers briefed on what he had uncovered regarding Sadler's past, then sent them out to fill in the blanks where they could.

They were reasonably successful. Enquiries quickly discovered that whenever he had returned to labouring jobs on land it had usually been with the East and West India Dock Company who owned a tea warehouse on Cutter Street, Houndsditch. They knew James Sadler reasonably well and confirmed they employed him from 1 December 1887 until the end of July 1888 on a casual labour basis, and again, on the same basis, in October 1888 until March of 1889. Diligent investigations also found Rose Moriarty, the woman Sarah Sadler said they had lived with back in 1880. She confirmed the story, and Sadler being employed at the time as a tram conductor, but insisted they had shared a house in 1878 not 1880. More importantly, for Swanson at least, she remembered the incident over the knife. According to her, it had not been a pocket-knife but a dagger of some sort. Sadler had used it to threaten his wife, though with no real intent and she agreed it had been removed and taken away by a woman but did not know who that woman had been.

Miss Duffield was also found. She remembered the two of them living with her ten years earlier. She was also able to confirm Sarah Sadler's story that she and her husband had briefly reconciled back in March 1889. There had been an accidental meeting between all three of them outside Whitechapel church. So, as far as Chief Inspector

Swanson was able to judge Sarah Sadler had told him the truth. Some of the dates were perhaps a little vague but he accepted that was to be expected. Who remembers in detail events from years earlier? What they do often remember though are those incidents where violence has been threatened, which probably made the incident with the knife of more interest than it otherwise would have been. If Sadler had threatened his wife, then clearly, he was used to handling such a weapon or so the argument probably went. But, for Swanson, the likely question was still: if he murdered Frances Coles could he have murdered all the rest?

The answer came after London docks confirmed that Sadler had returned to the sea after splitting with his wife and had continued to sail in the intervening three years. According to records, he had been at sea in the midsummer of 1888 returning to London on 1 October that year. The dock office also provided a list of the ships he had worked on after that date up until the Frances Coles murder:

Joined the SS Winestead 17 August 1888 returned London 1 October 1888

Joined the SS Bilboa 8 May 1889 returned London 7 July 1889

Joined the SS Loch Katrine 19 July 1889 returned London 1 October 1889

Joined the SS Alford 31 October 1889 returned Cardiff 27 May 1890

Joined the SS Chimborazo 16 June 1890 returned London 15 August 1890

Ship unknown but sailed to Amsterdam August 1890

Joined the SS Churton 15 September 1890 returned London December 1890

Joined the SS Fez to Turkey 24 December 1890 returned London 11 February 1891

Enquiries also ascertained that in between most of these sailings he had stayed at the Victoria Lodging House, Upper East Smithfield, where he was known to William Dann the lodging housekeeper, because he always paid one week in advance whenever he arrived. All of which meant that James Sadler, who in many respects fitted the Ripper profile, could not be the world-famous, Whitechapel murderer. Or at least not the killer stalking Whitechapel during August and September 1888. It was impossible to be at sea during the crucial murderous months of that year and killing Whitechapel's prostitutes at the same time. But it did not rule him out from being the killer of Frances Coles, which is what H Division's Leman Street police believed.

Enquiries from that point on centred on his movements throughout the night of 12 February and into the early morning of 13 February. Police now had a record of much of his background for the years that mattered so they could argue they knew the man, his occupation and how he had been living. What they now needed was to place him in Swallow Gardens and Arch 45 at the time of the murder. But that was going to prove far more difficult than they perhaps believed as they sifted through the detail of all that their enquiries had revealed.

But there was more to come, though not directly. Newspaper reporters had succeeded in locating James Sadler's mother. His wife, Sarah, had provided details that were more recent and pertinent, the state of their marriage, how the two had been living apart. What their editors wanted next were the details of his life before their marriage. Where had he come from? What was his upbringing? Why did he choose the sea? The more salacious the better probably. But what they stumbled across was simply a picture of everyday life in the East End.

Sadler's mother was 76 years old when they interviewed her and living in Walworth. The Elephant and Castle not too far away, which figured in the early years of his marriage. She was poor and still working, acting as nurse to a young child in her care and taking in sewing jobs to make a living. A widow, her husband, James Meal

Sadler, had died many years earlier of consumption, but had held down a well-paid job working as head clerk for a solicitor's practice at Lincoln's Inn Fields. According to her story, James had only been 3 when his father died, and the small family were then living in Stepney. She explained that her husband had a middle name, Meal, given to him at his baptism because a Captain Meal had been his grandfather. He was a wealthy man, who years before James's birth had been a part owner in several vessels sailing out of Yarmouth. But he was also a man who had endured a fair degree of sadness in his life, his wife being confined on a number of occasions to a Norfolk mental asylum where she eventually died. As to James's early working life, that had started as an under-clerk to the London docks and according to his mother not a job he ever enjoyed. The sea was his vocation. So, he stopped being a clerk and began to take work on the various steamers sailing out of London. Between voyages he did as he had done on occasion during his marriage, worked in the tea warehouses dockside. He also became a member of a Druids' lodge at Rotherhithe. A number of these lodges existed around London, similar in idea to the Free Masons but run in a different way. Some of these lodges existed on the basis that they operated in a philanthropic manner towards their members, offering benefits to those poorer members that occasionally found themselves in need. That could be why James joined. For a man making a living from the sea, where income was perhaps not always regular, maybe it paid to be a part of such an organisation. Not that it made any difference to Chief Inspector Swanson's ongoing investigation. They had, by this stage, reached a point where Sadler's past, interesting though it may be, made no impression on what was now important. With the Ripper, to their mind, out of the way, the timeline was all that mattered.

The hope, perhaps, that the post-mortem, which had been concluded by this stage, could add something more helpful was at best doubtful. That is not to say divisional surgeon doctor Dr Phillips, who conducted the post-mortem, was not thorough. On the contrary, he was probably extremely thorough. But, unlike today, a police and forensic science approach was non-existent. Therefore, there was little that would have been gleaned from the surgeon's report that would have aided Chief Inspector Swanson's case against James Sadler. However, it is of interest, or at least what there is of it, to modern eyes. Provided, of course, that it is accepted that this report, made at the time of his examination of the body, no longer exists, as far as anyone is aware. What we have available today comes from the various press reports made at the time. Nevertheless, there is enough to at least form an opinion as to how Frances met her death.

Frances Coles, remember, judged on that earlier press release, which is worth repeating, was 5ft tall (1.52m). She had brown hair, brown eyes, and wore a black dress, satin bodice and button boots. Found in the pocket of her dress were three pieces of black crepe, one old striped stocking and a comb. The clothes she wore were old, worn and in need of being cleaned and she had no money on her person when found. According to Frederick Oxley, the first doctor on the scene, when he examined her, he believed there was no blood on her clothes either. The only blood at the scene, according to his later report, was on the ground. One blood pool, which had clotted by the time he arrived, lay 1ft (0.3m) away from the body and, nearby, a stream of blood was running into the gutter opposite. He also believed, after his initial examination, she had sustained two cuts to her throat.

An examination carried out in the early hours of a winter morning without much external light is obviously never easy. That assessment by Dr Oxley of the wounds inflicted was wrong and corrected by Dr Phillips after his more thorough examination at the Montague Street mortuary. In his report to police and later testimony given in court, he stated that there were in fact three cuts to the throat: 'one from left to right, another from right to left, and a third from left to right.'

There were also marks on Frances Coles's chin which he believed had been made by fingernails, the implication being her assailant had held her chin at some point, perhaps in order to push it to one side, to allow him easier access to her throat. Contentiously perhaps, he also believed that marks or wounds to the back of her head indicated she had either fallen or been pushed back and on to the ground. The attacker, in his opinion, had then struck from her right side using the knife in his right hand to inflict wounds, possibly the ones that were made in a left to right manner, once she was on the floor.

Dr Oxley was less certain. He expressed the opinion that her attacker could have struck from the front. Both doctors agreed, however, after close examination of these wounds, that the knife used had not been particularly sharp and the killer had not exhibited a degree of skill in their execution. Just how two doctors could have arrived at that last conclusion is hard to fathom. Frances Coles clearly died as a result of an attack that was soundless, no noise made by either the attacker or the victim, and the wounds were deep. Blood loss, according to all reports, was great, all of which indicate a killer who knew exactly what he was doing and exactly how to strike. No blood was reported by police or medical men as being present on the nearby wall, though police did apparently mark the brickwork with a cross to indicate where, in their estimation, the attack had taken place. All blood loss appears to have been on the ground; Frederick Oxley's observations of the murder site, which seems to have been the only thorough record made, stated blood pooled away from the body. He is surely expressing an opinion (apparently readily accepted by Phillips), though perhaps not clearly enough, that she was on the ground when the left carotid artery was cut. The absence of blood on her clothes and no blood on the walls being the clearest indicators to substantiate Dr Oxley's view. Not that it made any difference to how the police saw the murder. According to numerous press reports they appeared to stick, initially, to the notion that the killer had struck from behind and that Frances Coles, inebriated after a night spent in the numerous pubs around Whitechapel, had been an easy victim. Though here their theory took a knock when Dr Phillips was able to show there was no alcohol in her stomach and no traces of alcohol abuse in the organs of her body.

These findings must have seemed odd at the time, given that at this stage of their enquiries the police believed they had unambiguous evidence of her having taken part in a heavy drinking session with the man they thought had killed her, James Sadler. But not odd enough to create doubt in their minds over Sadler's guilt; he was still held in custody with enquiries still ongoing. Obviously, what was needed was a more thorough forensic analysis of the confined area of Arch 45 to better understand the murder scene. Something, unfortunately, that in 1891 was simply not available to them.

It was also not possible. The murder site had never been properly protected by police. Within hours of their leaving, groups of young people, known locally as *match burners* because they would light their way through the centre of the arch by striking matches, invaded the arch. There they would play the detective or try to re-enact the murder. To them it was all a game, and Frances Coles another Ripper victim. They never doubted it. This mystical, mysterious man who had terrorised Whitechapel was back. According to various press reports, on the night following the murder, someone wheeled in a barrel-organ and crowds gathered to sing popular musical hall songs about *Jack*. Fame and notoriety had already placed him at the heart of local folklore. If there had been anything missed by that early morning police search, it was lost forever within hours of their departure.

Which means, of course, the problem we have today when sifting and evaluating the information available at the time is simply that it is scant on detail and more so in the case of the pathology. Just how deep were the cuts? Which cut was made first? What was the blood loss? Where precisely was it found? These are a few of the relevant questions – and of the murder site itself there are even more. For example, how exactly did this murder take place. In other words, how did the killer operate? Did he attack from the front? There was a suggestion that he had. Did the position of the body indicate the direction of the attack? Would it have been possible for her killer to have hidden beneath that archway? All relevant and crucial to understanding exactly what happened beneath Arch 45 at around 2.15 a.m. It is doubtful that any of these questions were ever raised. James Sadler, found so quickly after the murder, maybe altered the mindset of those involved in investigating the killing. They had a suspect, they had a knife, perhaps how he did it was unimportant.

As far as police were concerned at that stage of their enquiries and after the long, drawn-out interview with his wife, Sadler had to be their man, but was unlikely to be the Ripper. The next stage, as the police knew well enough, was to go back to the timeline. If they were to convict Sadler maybe the best way was to piece together Frances Coles's movements rather than his and then see how James Sadler fitted in.

Chapter 7

Frances

By the time of Chief Inspector Swanson's meeting with Sarah Sadler, police enquiries around the streets of Whitechapel and the various public houses that made up the district had begun to build a reasonably accurate time map. More information had come into Leman Street police station from locals who knew Frances Coles and who were able to add detail to the time map they were developing. By this stage of the enquiry, they knew she had been a regular at Shuttleworth's coffee house on Wentworth Street. Anne Shuttleworth, who ran the place with her husband, had told them that two or three weeks earlier Frances had fallen down steps outside the premises. According to Mrs Shuttleworth, that fall had been heavy and serious with damage to the back of her head and had necessitated a degree of attention just to stop the bleeding and get the wound bandaged up. That wound, she thought, may well have been the reason Dr Phillips saw blood on the back of her head. She questioned his reasoning that being pushed hard against the road when attacked caused it. Could it not be the old wound re-opening when her head struck the road when she fell?

Whether Dr Phillips concurred is doubtful. Certainly, nothing seems to have been mentioned by him or reported as such in the days following. But maybe there is merit in what Anne Shuttleworth had to say. There is no doubt she knew Frances reasonably well and that Frances visited her shop on a regular basis and at varying hours of the day. According to Mrs Shuttleworth, on the night of her murder Frances had been at the shop twice; the first time she was seen by herself, when Frances arrived at around 5.15 p.m. alone.

She was joined half an hour later by a sailor, a man wearing a peak cap and pilot coat, standard sailor wear; a man police now knew as James Sadler. The second, and by far the most interesting visit, was at 1.30 a.m. on 13 February. Anne Shuttleworth had, by that time, gone to her bed. At that hour of the morning the shop was being managed by local fish porter, Joseph Haswell, a man she employed, probably to do the late shift. According to what he had told her, and later the local police, Frances bought food, which she ate in the shop and paid for with one penny and two halfpennies (2d in total). She left at about 1.45 a.m. and headed off towards Brick Lane.

More information had also become known regarding the activity around Swallow Gardens and the thoroughfare that was Arch 45. Their own officers, constables Hyde, Hinton and Elliot, who had been patrolling sections of Royal Mint Street, had already agreed that movement through the area had been light throughout the night and virtually non-existent by around 2 a.m. They had already interviewed those that had been seen, including of course Kate McCarthy, Thomas Fowler, the Knapton brothers and William Friday. There were also a few others, all railway workers, but none had anything to add to what was already known. Then local enquiries unearthed Soloman Guthrie and Michael Raddy. Both passed through the arch at key times, Soloman at around 2.10 a.m., Michael at around 2.15 a.m. Neither saw anything of importance. But the timing is significant and contradictory when set against the observations made by the three constables because it questioned their cognitive abilities, although possibly not in any serious way. The beats they had been following on the night of the murder had been constructed in such a way that there were short periods of time when at least two of them, Hyde and Hinton, had moved off Royal Mint Street. But perhaps more importantly, their testimony, if these railmen were being truthful and accurate about the times, then cast doubt over PC Thompson's time of discovery as per his later report. If their recall was true, then where was he? Once through that arch it was a 30-yard walk, by the constable's own assessment, from the arch exit to Chamber Street. They never saw him. He never saw them. So, did he really hear the killer's footsteps, or did they belong to Michael Raddy?

It is an intriguing thought. It also raises many other questions about that night. But not apparently for the police. They had their man. What they probably hoped for was a better understanding of how his movements impacted on the events of that night; that would give them a better grasp of his perceived involvement in the night's events.

It is likely that at some point around the 19/20 February they held a meeting to assess all the information they had by now gathered, if for no other reason than to piece together Frances Coles's known movements in conjunction with Sadler's and plot for themselves a true timeline before the inquest re-sat. However, there was one piece of contentious evidence they would have been forced to deal with if that timeline was to be accurate. That of a woman named Ellen Calanna, alias Calman. A Whitechapel prostitute known to police and a woman who, on the morning of the murder, had walked into Leman Street police station and made a statement claiming to have met with Frances in the early hours of the morning just prior to her murder. This evidence had not yet been presented to the coroner's court and which, it is fair to say, had been largely ignored by the murder investigation team despite its apparent relevance.

Whether because they believed her story to be unreliable or simply that, to them, it was simply not credible, is not recorded. What is and perhaps explains their reluctance to act on it, is the fact she initially claimed the time of that meeting was around 3 a.m. Frances, of course was dead by that time, which understandably cast serious doubts on her account. By the time Ellen later returned to Leman Street police station to amend that time, claiming it was an error, that she had misremembered the time and it should have read as 2 a.m., the damage had already been done. It seems doubtful the significance of that change was ever passed on to the investigation team. If it was, there seems to be no documentary evidence to support that. Alternatively, it could just be that she was not believed.

So, what did Ellen Calanna or Calman have to say?

In her amended statement, she claimed she and Frances had met on Commercial Street not far from the Princess Alice public house. They had then walked towards its junction with Whitechapel High Street and there met a man she described in her statement as being short, with a dark moustache, shiny boots and blue trousers, 'just like a sailor'. He offered her (Ellen) money to go off with him. She refused, claiming she had been put off by how he looked, which had angered him. He suddenly became violent, assaulted her, tore her jacket, and hit her in the face. Then there was some sort of stand-off before he turned his attention towards Frances and offered her half a crown (2s 6d). That was enough money to pay for lodgings for more than a week. Frances accepted. Ellen protested. But the deal was done, and Frances left with the sailor. The two of them then turned right on to Whitechapel High Street and headed off towards the Minories.

Now all documentation related to this statement is missing, so the veracity of what was stated and later reported by various newspapers cannot be verified. The essence of her story comes from the press reports, which best reflect the story she had originally told police. It has the ring of truth about it though the timing of the meeting between the two of them is probably incorrect. Joseph Haswell's account of Frances being ushered out of Shuttleworth's coffee house at 1.45 a.m., if it is accurate, means a 2 a.m. meeting was unlikely. But, making some allowance for error, and Ellen had of course been drinking, it could be assumed that they actually met nearer 1.50 a.m. and the clock she heard, probably after Frances and the sailor had walked off, was striking two; an initial meeting some twenty-five minutes away from her own murder if we accept PC Thompson's timings. A sobering thought, particularly if the man she met was her killer.

A question for the police ought to have been, 'Was that man Sadler and did he have polished boots?'

Ignoring Ellen Calanna's account, as they seem to have done, regardless of its accuracy or otherwise was obviously a serious error. But useful or not at that early stage of the police enquiry, it would not have changed the need to create that accurate timeline to aid their understanding of France Coles's movements on the night of her death.

Whilst Sadler's own statement of events on the night of 12 February had been a little nebulous, there was no denying the pair of them had been drinking heavily. Find the pubs, find the route, match the times, seem to have been the criteria set by Superintendent Arnold and the officers of Leman Street police station. What they came up with, though never published, must have been along the lines of the following:

12/13 February 1891
Midday Frances Coles and James Sadler leave their lodgings on White's Row
12.00–2.00 p.m. Drinking in The Britannia, Dorset Road
2.00–4.30 p.m. Not known
4.30–5.00 p.m. Drinking in The Bell on Middlesex Street
5.15–6.00 p.m. Both Frances and Sadler eating in Shuttleworth's coffee house
6.00–7.00 p.m. Drinking in The Marlborough Head on Pelham Street, Brick Lane
7.00–8.00 p.m. Arrive at the bonnet shop in Bethnal Green
8.00–9.00 p.m. Not known
9.00–9.45 p.m. She and Sadler walk to lodging house on Thrawl Street and Sadler attacked and robbed on the street
10.00–10.30 p.m. Frances Coles arrives alone at lodging house on White's Row
11.00–11.30 p.m. Sadler also arrives at lodging house on White's Row

12.30 a.m.? Sadler thrown out
1.00 a.m. Frances Coles leaves White's Row lodging house
1.30 a.m. Frances Coles enters Shuttleworth's coffee house on Wentworth Road.
1.45 a.m. Frances told to leave coffee house because they were locking up
1.45–2.00 a.m. Frances meets with Ellen Calanna and both meet a sailor
2.15 a.m. Frances Coles is murdered in Swallow Gardens

A loose-fitting account based upon what was by this time known and understandably a little inaccurate but with sufficient information to allow police to trace her movements with a degree of accuracy; it also shows that a fair amount of alcohol had been consumed by both parties. A pub crawl that had started at midday and continued, with the odd break, until around nine o'clock at night. But it also raises questions. Frances was believed to have been inebriated at the time of her death and the number of public houses she and James Sadler visited would support that notion. Yet, according to Dr Phillips, there was no alcohol in her body when he conducted the post-mortem. It is fair to say we now understand much more about alcohol and how the body processes and eliminates it than anyone did previously, which makes that autopsy report all the more difficult to understand. Even if, as the above suggests, she stopped drinking at around 9 p.m., there ought to have still been alcohol in her system. According to modern science, the body is really efficient at moving one unit of alcohol out of the system every hour. So, drinking for around eight hours is going to take until well into the following morning for a body to rid itself of the alcohol. But in Frances's case there was none, and she was murdered within five hours of her last drink. Or was it a case that whilst she definitely took in alcohol, she did not consume the amount we are led to believe? Remember Frances was a streetwise young woman, her trade was prostitution, and it was probably more important to her that the man drank far more than she. The post-mortem findings suggest that whilst she may have taken in alcohol, she had not taken in enough to be drunk. In turn, that suggests when she walked into Arch 45, she was sober, in control, and less likely to have been taken by surprise than is assumed. Which makes her murder the harder to understand.

Does it matter? The answer must be yes. When Frances Coles was attacked, she was no easy target. At that time in the morning, borne out by Dr Phillips' examination, she was making rational decisions. So, if she went off with a sailor at 2 a.m. in the morning lured by the prospect of a half-crown piece, she knew what she was taking on. She also probably knew enough about the local topography to know what could or could not be done beneath Arch 45. It was a well-used thoroughfare and not necessarily the best place to carry out business despite the fact that it was common knowledge prostitutes did often make use of it. It was also a good fifteen- twenty-minute walk away from where she supposedly left Ellen Callana, if not more, and policed every twenty minutes or so at that time of night. After eight years plying a dangerous trade on the streets of Whitechapel, she would have known all this. So, did something else steer her in the direction of Swallow Gardens and was that something James Sadler?

Since the adjourned inquest, which had exposed the police's lack of knowledge over Sadler's movements after midnight on 13 February, those investigating the murder had been busy trying to fill in the gaps. It is likely that H Division's senior officers including inspectors Edmund Reid, and James Flanagan who had been involved in the case since the murder had been discovered, were all heavily involved. Certainly, evidence had been coming into the division throughout mid-February, which helped build a picture of Sadler's late-night movements. The problem they had was proving any of it put the sailor into Swallow Gardens at the crucial time, not that it seems to have rocked their conviction that, despite all this, he was still the killer. After Chief Inspector Swanson's interview with Sadler's wife, they had a comprehensive picture of his earlier life. They also had the testimony of Duncan Campbell who claimed Sadler had sold him the knife that the police were convinced Sadler had used to commit the murder. They also had that murder weapon and could now account for Sadler's movements on the key night up to a point where he was in the vicinity of that Archway. Whether Charles Mathews believed that was enough is not known but it would seem the police were satisfied it was.

Chapter 8

Proof

The resumed inquest on Friday, 20 February would test the theory. Coroner Wynne Baxter, 47 years old, lawyer by trade, knew that too. He was all too familiar with murder in the East End, police procedure and just how important the inquest verdict would be to their enquiries, particularly with a suspect in custody. His experience had been gained through his involvement in a number of high-profile murder cases, including those of Polly Nichols, Annie Chapman and Elizabeth Stride, considered by most to be Ripper victims. So, it is fair to say he grasped the importance of the case before him and just how it figured in the unsolved Whitechapel murder file of the previous decade. The significance of this court and the verdict of its unpaid jurors would influence any decision made by the public prosecutor's office with regard to James Sadler.

The task of the day, pre-set by the witness list in front of him, intended only to examine the timeline involving Sadler. This was to be the police case against their prisoner, an examination essentially of all the evidence they had gathered in support of their contention he had murdered Frances Coles. They wanted to be able to show he had been the only man Frances had encountered on the day she died who could have wielded the knife that killed her, that the two of them had been inseparable for much of it and that he had been at Swallow Gardens at the time of her death. The police were pretty much in charge of most of the evidence Wynne Baxter would hear, as much of it would come from their own officers.

How confident police were that it would be enough to convince a coroner's jury is perhaps debatable. If they had done their homework, then they must have realised before the court opened there were still difficulties to overcome, particularly when it came to that timeline; by this stage in proceedings Sadler also had good, sound legal representation. Any weakness was bound to be exposed, and it was.

From the outset there was contention. Legal representation for James Sadler made it inevitable. Unlike in the previous session, and the hearing before Mr Mead at the police court, this time witness testimony was to be challenged, particularly when trying to place Sadler in time and place. It had not been lost on his defence barrister that putting Sadler up against the clock only worked if witnesses to his movements owned one. Ambiguity was not acceptable. This, as he rightly knew, was essentially a murder trial under the guise of a coroner's court. If Sadler had committed murder and police were unable to place him at the scene with certainty, then they had to create opportunity. Timings throughout the night in question had to be accurate or shown to be false.

To that end, the inquest opened where the last had finished, hearing evidence of Sadler's movements during the early part of the night of the murder. The police had already established his movements as indicated in his own statement: the buying of the new hat found with the body; his late arrival at the lodging house in White's Row; and the mugging in Thrawl Street that had deprived him of his money. But other witnesses had, by now, come forward and these the coroner needed to hear.

The first was Anne Shuttleworth. Her evidence, volunteered to the police a couple of days earlier, stating Frances was in her coffee house twice on the night of the murder was challenged. Not over the number of visits but the timing of those visits. In the statement she had given, she claimed Frances had arrived alone at 5.15 p.m. Barrister, Mr Lawless queried that assertion. He wanted to know how she could be so certain. She said because Frances had looked at the clock when James Sadler came in and remarked it was a quarter past five. But, as the barrister pointed out, when she said that she was already sitting in the shop. He was right and Anne Shuttleworth then amended her statement and agreed Frances had arrived at 5 p.m. Head barman at the Bell was then called to testify. He told the court Sadler had arrived at his public house with Frances at around half past four and stayed until half past five. He remembered because of what Sadler had ordered at the bar: 'He called for a quartern of gin and cloves.'

Between the two of them they had made the point Lawless intended. The timings were not to be trusted. James Sadler could not have been in the coffee house and in the Bell at the same time. Point well made.

It set the scene for the rest of the day: challenge time and place.

Sarah Fleming, deputy of No.8 White's Lodge where Sadler and Frances had stayed the night prior to the murder and had attempted to stay on the night she died, was asked about the time Sadler was refused a bed. She told the court he had no money and had been turned out at around 11 p.m. The night watchman, Charles Guiver had already told police it was after midnight.

Sarah Treadway of the Marlborough Head public house insisted the two of them had been in her pub between 6 p.m. and 7 p.m., drinking gin and peppermint. Yet how could they have been if they only left the Bell at 5.30 and still had to call at the Shuttleworth's?

Confusion reigned. It must have been clear by this stage to both the coroner and the jury that there were no accurate timings around Frances's and James Sadler's movements on the night of 12 February, leastways not from those who shared the early part of the night with them. Doubt had been successfully sown. So how would the police fair?

They wanted to be able to show Sadler had been in the vicinity of Swallow Gardens at a time that would have at least created opportunity. They knew from the evidence gathered he had been on the docks in the early hours of the morning of 13 February and that he had walked from there in the general direction of the murder site. Their intention, therefore, was to produce the officers who were on duty on the night of the murder in order that they could substantiate their belief that Sadler's very presence in the vicinity was enough to cast doubt over his innocence.

The first officer to give evidence, PC William Bogan, was a part of a team of officers whose job was to patrol the dock area. Essentially, they were support police manning the dock gates and ensuring the area leading into the docks was safe through the early hours of the morning. Clearing away the inevitable drunks trying to return to their ships was a part of that duty. James Sadler, who he had seen that morning, fell into that category. According to his testimony, Bogan saw Sadler at a quarter past one on the morning of 13 February. He told the coroner that when he saw Sadler, the man was inebriated and lying down on the floor in front of the gateway of the main entrance to the London Dock, frustrated because he had been unable to get through the gates: 'He had a slight abrasion on the left eye.'

PC Bogan went on to say he had taken hold of him by the collar and lifted him back on to his feet. At which point the dock gates had opened and PC Sutton, the dock gate keeper, had walked over to explain his refusal to allow Sadler access. According to Bogan, at that point Sadler became abusive. He tried to get him to move away from the docks but as he was doing so, a group of labourers approached and, realising Sadler had no money, offered to pay for his bed for the night. Sadler, addled by drink and extremely argumentative, called the labourers 'Dock Rats', and no doubt threw in a few more choice words. They became angry. Bogan said at that point he walked away when he realised Sadler was not going to budge and a fight, which he claimed not to have seen, followed. According to Bogan, he next saw Sadler in conversation with Police Sergeant Westley-Edwards on Tower Hill at 2 a.m., which corroborated the sergeant's earlier evidence to the police court. At that time, Bogan told the coroner, Sadler was bleeding from a head wound and appeared to be complaining of sore ribs after being beaten by the dock labourers. Sadler, he told the court, had stayed in conversation with the sergeant for around ten or twelve minutes. Swallow Gardens, Bogan believed, lay about a three or four-minute walk away.

Dock gatekeeper, PC Sutton, then explained to the jury why Sadler had wanted access to the docks:

> When he first came he asked for the Impusa which was a vessel belonging to the same firm as the Fez (Sadler's ship), and which was lying side by side with the Fez. He was half drunk and said he had been in a scuffle in Brick-lane.

Obviously, strong enough grounds to support refusal of entry and presumably PC Bogan, to whom he had explained the rationale behind the decision, had concurred, otherwise no doubt there would have been some further discussion. Certainly, he made no attempt to step in and support Sadler at that point. Or perhaps it was not his decision to make. Either way, it was clearly what sparked James Sadler's vituperative attitude towards the labourers. An argument he was witness to, though took care not to be a part of. According to PC Sutton, the main protagonist in that group had been a man named John Dooley. It was he who had struck Sadler, knocking him to the ground where he struck his head against the gate's metal work as he fell, ending up with a bad head wound. The fight that followed appears to have been brief though Sutton had little to say about it. But the time? 'That would be a quarter or ten minutes to two.'

Sadler, chastened by events and somewhat bloodied by the fight, then apparently sloped off in the general direction of the Minories.

That brought him into contact with Police Sergeant Westley-Edwards. He told the coroner, as he had Mr Mead in the police court, though with a little more detail, how he had met Sadler within minutes of him leaving the dock, how he had examined Sadler's head wound, made a cursory check of his upper torso after he had complained of a pain in his ribs, and then consulted with PC Hyde who had joined him whilst he carried out the examination. Their decision at the end of all that to let him go. 'The direction he took was towards Swallow Gardens.' The sergeant thought the time to be around 2.10 a.m.

This was corroborated to some degree by Frederick Smith, an employee of Lockhart's Coffee Tavern, Tower Hill, who had watched the whole incident through the shop's window. He told the court as the day's session drew to a close, he thought it had been around five minutes to two when the officers first met up with Sadler and began their brief examination but could not verify the time Sadler walked away again.

So, at the end of all that evidence, there was still confusion. If the intention had been to present a cohesive, comprehensive account of the murder of Frances Coles, with James Sadler at its centre, it failed. All the evidence so far showed the police case was purely circumstantial and built around a timeline that lacked credibility. The movements of James Sadler throughout the night and in particular between 1 a.m. and 2.15 a.m., the supposed time of the murder, were confusing. It placed him in the dock area and around Tower Hill but did not place him on Royal Mint Street, or near to the access into Swallow Gardens. The police argument that he walked to Arch 45 after his encounter with Sergeant Westley-Edwards was purely circumstantial. Whether Wynne Baxter felt the same as he called an end to the day's proceedings and adjourned court is not known. But certainly, he must have noted it. There can be no doubt Charles Mathews did. For him, as public prosecutor, the question of time was paramount. He must have realised at that juncture, as he probably had the last time, if this went to trial, he would need to be able to show, without question or legal challenge, exactly where Sadler was in relation to the murder site. If he could not do that with certainty, then the case would flounder.

There was clearly still work to be done if they were to make a better impact in the resumption set for 23 February.

Chapter 9

Review

Headquarters of H Division on Leman Street must have been the centre of fevered activity after the adjourned inquest. It was where the key players in this murder investigation were based and from where all investigations had been carried out. Under the overall control of divisional head, Superintendent Thomas Arnold, working alongside inspectors Henry Moore and Edmund Reid, and the guiding hand of Chief Inspector Donald Swanson who, though not based in Leman Street, spent a considerable amount of time sharing information with all three.

In 1891 it is fair to say they were the dream team. Moore had taken over as lead detective investigating the Whitechapel murders from Frederick Abberline back in 1889. The man, whose name today is synonymous with that of the Ripper, was at the start of a career that would take him from Whitehall to Scotland Yard and was an accomplished and dedicated detective. Edmund Reid had been heavily involved in every Whitechapel murder since joining H Division back in August 1888, and Donald Swanson had a reputation envied across the world. He had been brought in by Commissioner Charles Warren to oversee all investigations into Whitechapel's murders shortly after Reid's appointment, and he had been involved in every Ripper case. Whitechapel had become his domain and his reputation for success a positive. Although by this stage of the Ripper enquiry, his reputation was maybe not as impressive as it had been at the outset. Three years on and nothing to show probably tended to dampen enthusiasm in his detecting abilities. Nevertheless, his past record of high achievement was impressive.

High-profile cases had brought him to the attention of both the media and the highest echelons of the police over the years, resulting in deserved promotion and prestige. Cases that included the disappearance of the Earl of Crawford's body in 1881, one of Scotland's strangest cases; the Kingston murder of 1881; and the arrest of Percy Lefroy Mapleton for the Brighton railway murder – famous because his was the first murder where a composite picture of the killer had been put together and used on a wanted poster. There were other cases too: the Middlesbrough murder of Mary Cooper in 1884; the recovery of the Countess of Dudley's jewels after they had been stolen by Michael Davitt from the platform of Paddington Railway Station in December 1874; and many more – all of which had ensured his reputation for success amongst his peer group was both envied and respected.

His involvement in the Frances Coles murder must have fostered belief in some quarters at the outset of the case that her murder was far more important than it would have otherwise been. In turn, that fostered the suspicion in some quarters that James Sadler, if guilty, could also be the Whitechapel killer of the previous decade; a belief already expressed by some high-ranking police officers and supported by a number of London newspapers, even if not by the prevailing evidence.

So, there can be little doubt all the resources of Leman Street police had been aimed at proving in Wynne Baxter's court that James Sadler had committed the murder of Frances Coles. They had never looked in any other direction. Reputations were at stake. Therefore, it must have rung alarm bells that at this stage of the inquest all was clearly not going well. Nothing police had presented to the coroner so far helped prove their case. The evidence given to date was not only circumstantial but ineffectual. To argue that James Sadler had committed the murder beneath Arch 45 would only be valid if there were sufficient grounds to make such a claim. But what they had only shown was that he had been in the dock area in the early hours. More importantly perhaps, to the coroner's jury at least, they had also shown he was drunk and incapable. An unintentional alibi of their own making, caused, inadvertently, by the success of their enquiries into locating the public houses Sadler and Frances Coles had visited on the night of her murder. From that evidence alone, which was necessary to build the all-important timeline, it had become clear the man in the dock could well have been rendered incapable of committing any murder anywhere at that time of a morning. Of course, it did raise the question of whether or not Sadler really was that drunk at two o'clock in the morning after losing all his money on Thrawl Street earlier that same night? But in light of the testimony of their own officers, which had suggested he was, the question was never going to be asked. This was probably not lost on barrister, Mr Lawless, who must have realised at that point the case against James Sadler was beginning to crumble. But he would also have known there was still the knife.

For the police case this had to now be the key. Police had found the murder weapon, or so they believed, and the man who bought it from James Sadler the morning after the murder. If the medical men who conducted the post-mortem agreed in court that it could have inflicted the wounds, then possibly that would be enough to convince the coroner's jury that their arrest of Sadler had been justified. At this stage of proceedings, there was little else they could produce that would add credence to their case. The argument could only be that if the knife had belonged to James Sadler, and if it had been used to kill Frances, then stated times no longer mattered. The problem for them back in 1891, unlike today, they had no way of proving it. Useful blood analysis would not be available until the 1920s, therefore they were unable to tell from whom it came – that is if any blood had remained. Remember the knife had been washed before being sold on, which even today could have rendered it useless as far as forensic evidence is concerned.

There was also James Sadler's statement made within hours of the murder's discovery. It is clearly inaccurate. There was no serious, clear chronology to what he had told Donald Swanson in his interview at Leman Street police station, neither had he been concise in recalling his movements on the day of Frances's death. He had been vague, missed out key facts and misremembered events. Perhaps police really ought to have considered the question of his inebriated state on the night of the murder, long before the inquest ever opened.

Chapter 10

Resumption

This question was not going to be answered by Coroner Wynne Baxter's re-opened inquest on Monday, 23 February. But the belief that James Sadler's drunken state was genuine raised its head from the outset. Coffee house waiter, Charles Littlewood, who had been on the early morning shift at his shop on Whitechapel Road, told the court that Sadler walked into his business at half past six on the morning after the murder. He ordered cocoa, kept himself to himself and sat quietly in a corner. According to Mr Littlewood, Sadler ordered a second cup about an hour later but was refused service because he appeared to be drunk. Apparently, he made no protest, which, considering his belligerent attitude hours earlier, seems somewhat out of character. He left the shop at about half past seven, blood stains noticeable on his left wrist and apparently more sober than when he had walked in.

But Littlewood's testimony was challenged by his manager, Stephen Longhurst. A man who, to police satisfaction, identified Sadler as certainly being that early morning customer but not that he left around half past seven but more like eight-thirty or nine o'clock; something not missed by Sadler's barrister Mr Lawless, sowing yet more seeds of doubt around the timing of events in the hours surrounding the murder.

The only real clarity came from Joseph Haswell who reprised his evidence, given to the police days earlier, about seeing Frances Coles, alone and obviously hungry, in Shuttleworth's eatery at half past one in the morning, buying food and not leaving until around a quarter to two. As far as can be ascertained from recorded inquest details, Haswell does not appear to have been challenged, no doubt because he told the court he had to lock up the shop at that hour. He was an employee. It was accepted he would know what time to open and what time to close. He was also familiar with Frances and her nocturnal habits. So, his assessment of time was probably reasonably accurate.

Not that it helped the police when it came to proving Sadler's guilt. According to available evidence, they had always known the two of them had not been together between around midnight and two o'clock in the morning. But then, as they believed the evidence would show, there had been a meeting somewhere in the vicinity of that archway and they thought they could prove it. Not by any sighting of the attack, obviously, but simply by Sadler's ownership of that knife and that knife being the murder weapon.

The main act of the day, to use a theatrical term, was Duncan Campbell, the sailor who had bought it from him. A man police probably hoped would swing that jury verdict their way, when he took the stand. His testimony was clear, concise and did not deviate from his earlier police statement. James Sadler, he told the coroner, walked into the Sailors' Home on Well Street at about 10.15 a.m. on the morning of the murder (Friday, 13 February). It was a place Sadler would have been familiar with and a place he had perhaps used on occasion; an impressive-looking four-storey building opened back in 1835, which offered board and lodgings for sailors who could pay. Self-contained in many ways, it had its own bank, acted as a post office, had an on-site medical officer and a central space where sailors of all nations could meet and spend time together. Campbell had obviously used it before and seemed very familiar with its services and surroundings. Sadler, he told the court, approached him as he went to sit by the fire. It was a cold February day, and it was the warmest place to be. 'I'm nearly dead. I've been out all night, and I've got robbed. I'm dying for a drink,' were Sadler's first words when the two men met. It opened up a conversation about money, or rather James Sadler's lack of it. The sailor, according to Duncan

Campbell's re-telling of his story, obviously needed to raise cash and took a knife from his pocket and offered it up for sale. There appears to have been no bartering. Campbell obviously liked the look of the knife and offered him 1 shilling and a quantity of tobacco, which Sadler readily accepted. He described it as a pocket-knife, with a *big blade,* and after opening out the blade realised it had not been made in England, which he pointed out to Sadler who told him, 'I bought it abroad … in America.'

Not that it seemed to make too much difference to Campbell who waited until Sadler had left before making any further detailed examination. Then, later that day, he told the coroner, after hearing about the murder at Swallow Gardens he took the knife with him into a nearby lavatory. There, he made a much closer inspection in private, presumably because news of the killing had raised his suspicions. What he found after washing raised them even more. 'The water in which I had washed the knife was slightly discoloured.'

Reasonably enough he was pressed by the coroner to explain that observation with a little more clarity, and he explained that by discoloured he meant the water had turned a salmon colour, which had concerned him. Obviously not enough, because twenty-four hours later he, like James Sadler, then used it to raise money for himself. Though, he was at great pains to explain, only because he had not been able to access funds through the bank at the Sailors' Home, it being Saturday and the bank closed. So, he decided to use the knife as collateral and pawn it; nothing unusual in that given the time and place and it was something he had done before with the proprietor of the shop opposite, Thomas Robinson, who he was confident would be willing to make him an offer. A deal was struck. The knife sold for 6d, which obviously suited Campbell with a redemption value of 9d should he want to buy it back.

However, he told the coroner, conscience had got the better of him when he realised the knife could have been used to murder Frances Coles, and by implication James Sadler could have been the man wielding it. So, on the following day, he walked to Leman Street police station and told them what he suspected:

> After a bit I was taken downstairs into a room lighted with gas. There were fifteen or sixteen men in that room. They were mostly dressed as seamen. I was told to pick out the man who had sold me the knife. The men were arranged in a semi-circle, and in the extreme corner I saw the man. I saw the scar on his head, which I had noticed on Friday morning.

He and Sadler had never met before, so the scar was obviously the only thing he seemed to recognise, not the man. He was pressed on the time of Sadler's arrival in the Sailors' Home. The time he had given, 10.15 a.m., Lawless thought to be vague. Campbell, he postulated, had not consulted a clock and his selection of Sadler from the police line-up, he argued, had been less than confidently done, with only the scar on his head being used to confirm identity. There were other sailors on the streets of London that day, he pointed out to the jurors, who could well have matched the same description. Doubt and mistrust, up to this point, had proven effective in Sadler's defence and Lawless had employed it well. But Campbell, unmoved by the barrister's scepticism, seems to have been quite clear, at least in his own mind. The knife he had bought had definitely come from Sadler's hand and their meeting had been around 10.15 a.m., contentious or not.

It was also supported, to some degree, by evidence from Edward Jerrand Delaforce, described by the *Southend Standard*, which reported much of this hearing, as being the delegate superintendent at the shipping office, Tower Hill. Evidence had already been heard from staff at the lodging house in White's Row, that Sadler had tried to buy a bed on the night of the murder by offering up a statement of earnings. What Delaforce brought to the hearing was testimony that Sadler presented the same statement at his counter on the same morning as that meeting with Campbell and supposedly only minutes later: 'It was at half past ten. He presented a wages account, on which was the name of "T. Sadler". The amount was for £4 15s 1d.'

For Lawless, it was important to either discredit Duncan Campbell's version of events or at the very least show the time he claimed the meeting had taken place to be inaccurate. The walk from the Sailors' Home to the shipping office was about five or six minutes. If Campbell could not be precise about the time Sadler had arrived or left, but the shipping office could, there was cause for doubt. Simple principle. If there had been debate over selling of the knife initially and a conversation in front of a warm fire, then there had to be doubt that the man who sold the knife had been James Sadler, particularly if the time of 10.15 was proven to have been wrong and the time had been much later. It was a valid point and Lawless was no fool. He must have realised that if Campbell's evidence was accepted without question by the jury as a truth, then it raised questions over the veracity of Sadler's police statement. When he made it on 14 February, he made no mention of owning a knife or of ever having visited the Sailors' Home. According to Sadler, Campbell's story was a pure fabrication, and it may have been. But as Lawless quickly realised, he was never likely to discredit the old sailor's account in a coroner's court. All he could do was cast doubt as to its veracity, which he did, and hope the jury accepted his scepticism.

Doctors Oxley and Phillips wound up the day's proceedings with a perfunctory overview of the post-mortem and their initial assessment of Frances Coles's body in situ. Dr Oxley repeated his assertion that when he examined her beneath Arch 45 her clothes were in perfect order; there had been no blood on them, and the blood found on the floor had been about 1ft away from where she lay. He also agreed with police that the knife offered up by Duncan Campbell could have been used to inflict the wounds on her neck. He was challenged by Mr Lawless to tell the court whether the knife, if blunt, could have made the wounds and whether a man under the influence of alcohol could have wielded it. Dr Oxley was unsure:

> Well, I should think if it were much higher it would not have been able to do so. In my opinion the throat was cut when she was lying on the ground, and by a person who was in front of her. In my judgement a person incapably drunk could not have caused the wound, but a person who had been drinking might.

Dr Phillips concurred and, as he had stated in his police report, the killer had held her chin in his left hand to facilitate at least some of the cuts and had been right-handed: 'there were three distinct passings of the knife across the woman's throat – one from left to right, another from right to left, and the third from left to right again.'

At that point Wynne Baxter adjourned. There was still a lot to ponder.

Chapter 11

Funeral

It had been twelve days since the murder of Frances Coles by the time the funeral procession that would carry her body to the East London Cemetery gathered outside the mortuary in Mile End Road. James Coles, her father, had travelled from the Bermondsey Workhouse with his daughter Mary Ann. Between the two of them there was little money. In James's case, a combination of old age and unemployment had curtailed his earnings capability and kept him in poverty for years. As for his daughter, work had never paid enough to enable her to set money aside to help keep her father out of the hands of the Board of Guardians. So, what by this time, had become a lavish, expensive, highly visible funeral, had accrued a cost far beyond what either could afford. A cost met, after consultation with James Coles, by money raised from a fund set up by a number of philanthropic organisations: The Bartholomew Club; the Free Masons Lodge of Instruction 781; the Common Lodging House Mission; and Lady Ashburton, who in her later life had given money to, and supported, a number of Christian or welfare-driven organisations in London. It had proven to be a successful liaison. All these institutions readily accepted the Coles's financial situation, along with the dreadful circumstances of Frances Coles's death, and raised money from amongst their own supporters to ensure a woman who had little wealth or standing in life would exhibit both in death.

There were three horse-drawn mourning carriages: father and daughter in the first; institution heads in the second; and what was reported by the press as being an honorary solicitor, Mr Paynter, in the third. The hearse they all followed bore the polished elm coffin of Frances, a brass plaque attached giving her name and her age as 26. The latter was wrong, of course, her age being nearer 31 but was possibly based on information given to the funeral parlour by the police, rather than the family. Not that it mattered to the 500 mourners who flanked the cortège on each side acting as escort for the 5-mile journey to the cemetery.

At Whitechapel Church, the long procession paused. It was a little after two o'clock in the afternoon. The day was mild, a bright sky offering up a warm sun. Spring-like, was how *The Standard* reported it later that day. The passage of the cortège brought people out of their homes, from their work, stopped traffic and caused huge crowds. In places, the roadway as far as the eye could see was lined by people all of whom wanted to be a part of the day, pay their own respects, and perhaps reflect for a moment on a life they hadn't known but most certainly would have understood.

Those crowds never lessened as the slow journey progressed. By the time the cortège arrived at the cemetery, numbers had swelled to around 20,000. They filled the cemetery grounds, thronged around the graveside, and swamped the two police officers who had been sent to monitor the funeral. An ineffective police presence because they had underestimated local sentiment, perhaps failing to fully grasp the sense of anger or upset, or both, over what many people saw as their failure. The public had been living with the threat posed by the unresolved Whitechapel murders for four years, and for many attending that day, Frances was yet another unnecessary victim. If they needed any reminders of that earlier murder spree, as a number of newspapers pointed out, the grave of Frances Coles was within yards of four of those earlier victims: Mary Ann Nicholls, who had been murdered at the end of August 1888, Annie Chapman, in September, Elizabeth Stride, end of the same month, and Mary Jane Kelly in November. So, Frances was, strange as it may seem, in the company of women who may have met their deaths at the hands of her own killer. A thought probably not lost on a number of those gathered around the graveside that afternoon.

Of course, not all would have shared in the sentiment. A portion of that huge crowd was there because Frances was famous by association; murdered in Whitechapel, the manner of her death, her known occupation and her streetwise lifestyle gave her an unwarranted notoriety. There were some there that day who simply wanted a vicarious share in that experience, not that it would have mattered to the Coles family. For them, no matter how she had lived her life, she was a daughter, a sister, a member of the family, a loss. Would they have paid much attention to the connection her death had with any of the nearby graves? For them, the Reverend Thomas's prayer calling on the Almighty, 'to bring to the bar of justice the cruel hand that smote the death blow', was all that mattered. They, like that crowd, wanted justice for the victim he had just consigned to an earthly grave.

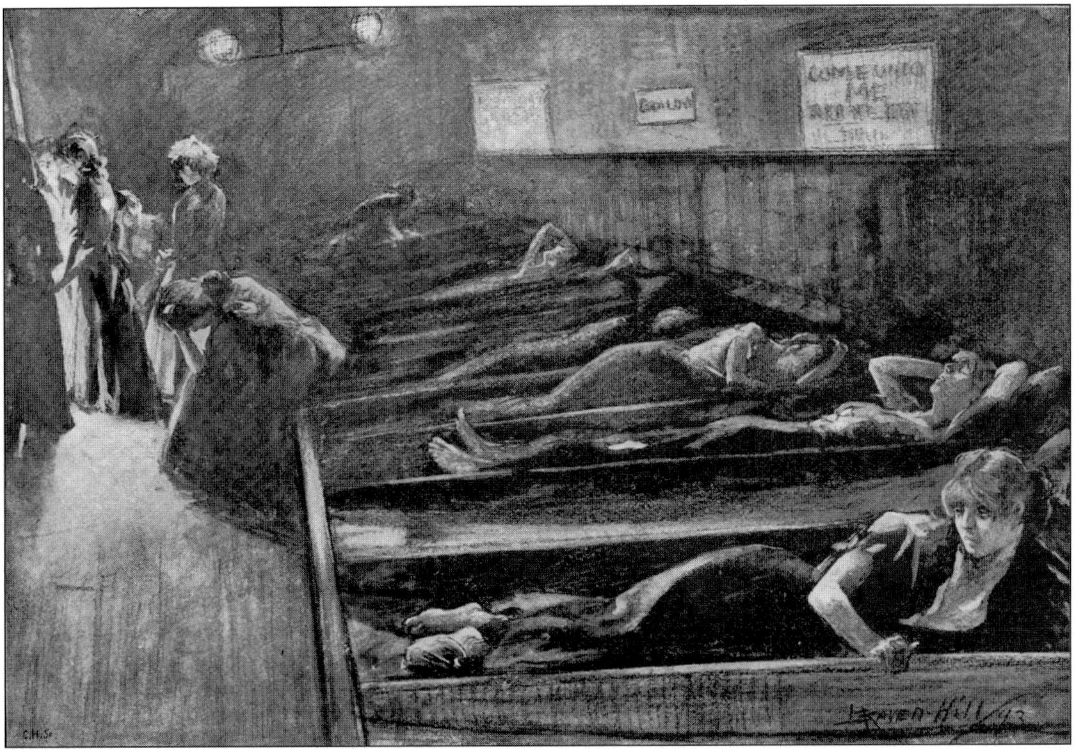

Above: East End doss house. (*Mary Evans Picture Library*)

Below: Victoria Home Lodging House, c.1900. (*Mary Evans Picture Library*)

VICTORIA HOME (WHITECHAPEL) : KITCHEN.

Above left: Outside of 3 Miller's Court, 1890. (*Mary Evans Picture Library*)

Above right: Whitechapel Lodging house, c.1890. (*Mary Evans Picture Library*)

Below: Whitechapel Workhouse casual ward, c.1900. (*Mary Evans Picture Library*)

Above: Engraving of Frances Coles. (*Alamy*)

Below left: Lyttleton Stewart Forbes Winslow. (*Alamy*)

Below right: Chief Inspector Donald Swanson. (*Alamy*)

Above: Whitechapel High Street. (*London Met Archive*)

Left: Commercial Street and Spitalfields Market. (*London Met Archive*)

Scotland Yard.
(*Author's collection*)

Wentworth Street,
c.1900. (*Author's
collection*)

Wentworth Street/
Petticoat Lane,
c.1900. (*Author's
collection*)

Left: Drawing of Frances Coles. (*The Penny Illustrated Paper*)

Below left: Murder site of Elizabeth Stride. (*Author's collection*)

Below right: James Thomas Sadler. (*Author's collection*)

SCENE OF THE BERNER STREET MURDER.

THOMAS SADLER THE WHITECHAPEL SUSPECT.

SCENE OF THE MITRE SQUARE MURDER,
AND MAP OF THE LOCALITY, SHOWING
POSITION OF THE SIX MURDERS.

Mitre Square murder site. (*Author's collection*)

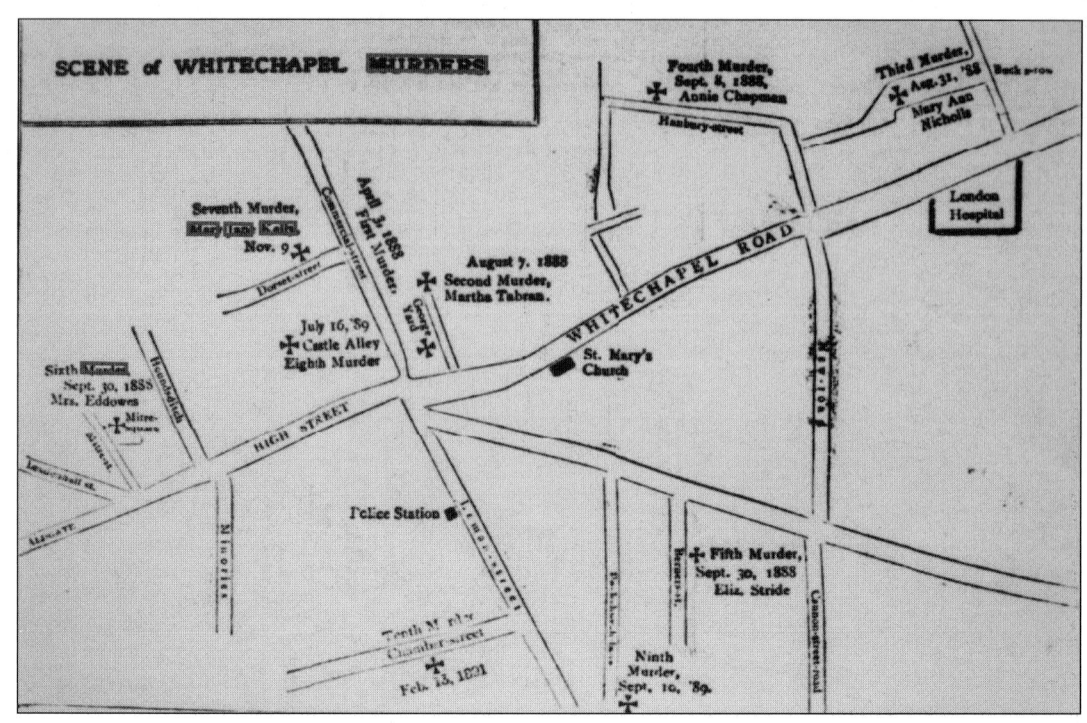

Above: Map of Jack the Ripper murder sites. (*Author's collection*)

Left: How the press sensationalised Jack the Ripper. (*Author's collection*)

ANOTHER

LONDON HORROR.

A WOMAN MURDERED IN DAYTIME IN WHITECHAPEL.

FIENDISH MUTILATION.

THE ANONYMOUS THREATS CARRIED OUT

INTENSE EXCITEMENT.

POST-MORTEM EXAMINATION OF THE WOMAN'S REMAINS.

PROCLAMATION BY SIR C. WARREN.

NUMEROUS ARRESTS.

INQUEST.

DETAILS AND VERDICT.

Chapter 12

Alice McKenzie

It is likely that as that funeral was winding its way along the streets of Whitechapel, Mr Charles Mathews, representative of the Treasury at the four adjourned inquests, had by now already re-examined the case against Sadler. The last adjournment, at the end of what had been a better day for the police case, had caused less anxiety than the previous sitting – mainly due to the positive testimony heard by the coroner, particularly that of Campbell and the buying of the knife which had been far more compelling. Place and time were also far less contentious. Not that they alone would erode the faults and inaccuracies of evidence that had already been heard, but it perhaps reinforced his belief in Sadler's guilt, even though it must have still been self-evident that the police case had a problem. This was contrary to what he had initially believed would be the case when he took his seat on the first day of this protracted inquest.

For him, at that point as a representative of the crown prosecution service, the police evidence against Sadler back then had no doubt appeared to be solid. They had the man, they had the timeline, they had the weapon. All that had been needed was to hear the evidence that would place him at the murder scene and a jury verdict declaring him to have been the murderer. A quick follow-up at the police court, due process, and then the Old Bailey for an easy murder trial. Unfortunately, as he sat in his office after Wynne Baxter's adjournment, Mathews was probably trying to understand just how difficult it had become to reach that verdict and how inconsistent police evidence against James Sadler was proving to be. Essentially, their own officers were conflicted on time, as was everyone else he had listened to. No one had been able to sow the seeds of doubt over the sailor's movements in that key part of the early hours of 13 February. What they had done, particularly with regards to the police evidence, was highlight the difficulty any future jury would have in accepting Sadler could have been wielding his knife at 2.15 a.m. beneath Arch 45 at Swallow Gardens. Clearly, by their own testimony the man had been drunk, incapable, and too injured to have inflicted the wounds suffered by Frances Coles. Or that is how it probably seemed. The verdict needed was slipping away because they had failed to be objective in the way they had presented their own case. More work had to be done.

All he was certain of at that point, was that James Sadler was not the Ripper. The one thing Inspector Moore and his team seemed sure of is that in 1888, at the time of the Whitechapel murder spree, Sadler had been at sea. But there was Alice McKenzie.

Police had run a check on the ships Sadler had sailed on and the dates on which they had sailed. From that, they deduced that back in 1888 he could not have been involved in the Ripper crimes, which is why he had been discounted as the Whitechapel murderer. But there had been one other victim besides Frances Coles, and that was Alice McKenzie some nineteen months earlier. Sadler's discharge papers had shown he had joined the SS *Loch Katrine* on 19 July 1889. Alice had been murdered two days earlier, 17 July, just before 1 a.m. in similar circumstances to those of Frances Coles.

H Division's PC Walter Andrews had found her body at 12.50 a.m., lying on the pavement in Castle Alley, off Whitechapel High Street. In his later report, he stated the exact time as being, 'ten minutes to 1 o'clock', and added that he had touched her, and her body was still warm. She had suffered two cuts to her throat: one more of a stab wound, the other a cut. Blood had pooled beneath her head and, according to a medical examination made whilst her body was still in situ, she had fallen on to her face and then been turned on to her back to inflict the second of the two wounds, the killer being on her right side. The position of the body was confirmed by the testimony of Sergeant Badham, who joined the constable within minutes of him blowing his whistle, his statement making it clear that when found she had been lying on her right. He also noted that her skirt had been pulled up to her waist exposing her abdomen where horizontal cuts had been made, none of which had penetrated the body cavity – possibly an attempt at some sort of mutilation. The murder weapon was judged to have been a knife of some sort.

Her description, later issued to the press, was widely publicised in the hope it would aid identification: 'Hair and eyes brown, complexion pale, dressed in red stuff dress, sleeve patched with maroon, brown stuff skirt, brown linsey petticoat, odd stockings (one red and the other maroon), white chemise and apron, button boots, and paisley shawl.'

Not that it was needed. Local to the area and well-known, she was quickly identified by casual market labourer, John McCormack. The two of them had been living together for about six years. According to his later statement, she had been working as a washerwoman for the nearby Jewish community and not as a prostitute. However, he admitted there could have been occasions when she had taken to the streets and worked as such, but not in recent times as far as he knew. He put her age at around 40.

Others claimed they had known her by different names, Bryant, Kelly and Murrell being the most common. Although just how recent they had been in use, or why, was never fully explored. For police, who knew many of the street prostitutes, having another alias, just as Frances Coles had, was far from uncommon in Whitechapel. Not that any of that helped understand why she had wandered into the alley in the early hours of a rainy Wednesday morning.

Margaret Franklin, who lived on Flower and Dean Street, came forward within hours of the body's discovery and added a little more background information. She had known Alice for some fourteen or fifteen years and told police she knew Alice had often been in the company of a blind man, though did not know where he lived. She knew little else other than Alice McKenzie's life had been hard, like most others living in Whitechapel, though generally stable. Certainly not bad enough, she thought, to have taken to the streets at night working as a prostitute – although she did qualify that statement by adding that perhaps there had been aspects of Alice's life she had been unaware of. The same could probably be said of most living in the area. What police were more interested in was the fact Margaret claimed to have seen Alice just an hour or so before she was murdered, hurrying along Brick Lane. The two of them had even exchanged a few words, but Alice said she had no time to stop, and she remembered the shawl. It had just started to rain. The direction of travel suggested she was not heading home, which was a shared room at a lodging house on Gun Street, and she was sober. This was important to the developing investigation because Alice, according to those that knew her, liked a drink. Her reason for not stopping to chat to a woman she knew well suggested she had a place she needed to be. The question for police was why Castle Alley? The same question would be posed about the murder nineteen months later in Swallow Gardens.

Very much a working area and poorly lit at night, the alley itself was some 500ft long and around 30ft wide, so a fairly narrow space. Access was generally gained via a covered passage only wide enough for two people to pass each other just off Whitechapel High Street, one of three ways in or out. A second entrance ran from Wentworth Street past what was known as the Board school, which projected out into the roadway narrowing that entrance to about 18 feet. The third way in or out was accessed from nearby Newcastle Street. This is important only because there were three police officers on duty at the time of the murder: PC Andrews, who approached from Whitechapel High Street and two of his colleagues patrolling Wentworth Road. The only way out therefore, for Alice's killer, was via that third exit.

Extremely dark at night, Castle Alley was initially reported as having only one streetlamp, beneath which, strangely enough, the murder had been committed. It was also littered with a jumble of hand carts, tradesmen's vans, and costermongers' barrows with only a narrow sidewalk open to pedestrians – in many ways a similar setting to that beneath Arch 45.

Divisional police doctor Phillips and a Dr Bond, who helped carry out the post-mortem, were divided in their opinions on the notion that she had been murdered by the Ripper. Dr Phillips felt the wounds to the neck were different from those seen on the previous year's victims and the wounds to the abdomen had not caused the kind of damage that would have been expected. Dr Bond disagreed. He thought she had been murdered by the same hand that struck terror into Whitechapel the year before. Castle Alley, some argued, was ideal Ripper territory as it was quiet at that time of night. It also offered easy escape and any killer standing at its heart, despite the light from a well-placed gas lamp, would not be seen by any police officer coming into the alley from any of the three access points. But they would have been heard, which was why there were no serious mutilations; no time to carry them out once alerted by the sound of PC Andrews' boots hitting the wet cobbles. Jack the Ripper, as far as the press and local opinion went, could not, therefore, be so easily discounted. Was there not a similar argument mounted over the murder of Elizabeth Stride and the later murder of Frances Coles?

The answer of course is yes, which meant for police investigating Alice McKenzie's murder the questions were always going to be the same and the results no different. This killer had committed murder in a place virtually surrounded by police and simply walked away. Just as he had when PC Ernest Thompson heard those footsteps disappear into the distance at the far end of Chambers Street. Whether that meant James Sadler, a disputed Ripper suspect, or another hand had been responsible was still to be decided.

Back in July 1889, of course, police knew nothing of the future murder to come. What knowledge they did have came from the multiple murders committed during the summer and early winter of 1888. Understandably, it clouded their judgement. In turn, that meant the investigation into Alice McKenzie's murder followed a familiar pattern which seemed to accept her killer was the same man who had used a knife against six previous victims: Martha Turner (Tabram), Polly Nicholls, Annie Chapman, Elizabeth Stride, Catherine Eddowes and Mary Jane Kelly.

This was an added pressure to a CID force still reeling from the public's criticism of its handling of those earlier cases and of their growing belief none of them would ever be solved. But those earlier investigations, unproductive as they were, had also brought about positive change. Crime scenes were better protected, more officers were brought in to oversee enquiries and the scope of those enquiries widened. There was also more acceptance of the theory that whoever the killer was, his escape via London's docks to the sea was credible. So, within hours of the discovery of Alice's body, instructions had been issued to the East End Thames Police to launch an intensive search of all shipping in the docks area, which resulted in all passenger vessels being boarded and searched for stowaways under the watchful eye of Detective Inspector Regan, who would repeat the exercise a year or so later. Crew lists, maintained by all vessels, were also checked in an attempt to verify the identity of any sailor on board any ship about to leave the dockside. Enquiries were widened further to include the residents of a hotel in Poplar, when it became known the chairman of the Whitechapel Vigilance committee, an organisation set up at the height of the Ripper murders back in 1888, had received a 'Jack the Ripper' letter. Initially, police ascribed no credibility to its contents when he first alerted them to its existence, it being one of many received both by themselves and the press over the previous months. It hinted at a Poplar hotel housing sailors resting between voyages being a temporary home to the Ripper and a probable July murder. The hotel was eventually named by various newspapers as the Eastern. The search of course, whether thorough or not, yielded nothing but did obviously reaffirm that seagoing killer theory.

By the mid-point of the month, the blind man Margaret Franklin had spoken of had also been identified and located. He was George Dixon, who rented a room at 29 Star Street, off Commercial Road.

He confirmed having been in company with Alice on the night she died. The two of them had been drinking in a pub near the Cambridge Music Hall, in Shoreditch. For how long he could not say, but whilst in there, according to his later statement, he claimed to have heard Alice ask someone if they would stand a drink and the reply was 'yes'.

The response cut short his night out because, he told police, after Alice accepted the offer, she walked him back to her lodging house in Gun Street and left him there. He presumed she then returned to the pub and probably the man who had paid for the drink. Who the man was, whether she returned to the same public house, or what she did for the rest of the night remained a mystery. Police enquiries, it would appear, uncovered nothing more of significance to the investigation. Nor did they come up with any reasonable explanation as to why she was in a hurry when Margaret Franklin saw her in Brick Lane.

Mr Wynne Baxter opened the inquest, held once again at the Working Lads' Institute, Whitechapel Road, on the afternoon of 18 July. Essentially this was to confirm identity, as protocol demanded, but there was some interesting information from the man Alice had shared a room with, John McCormack. According to his testimony, they had been living at the lodging house in Gun Street for about a year. On the night she died he had last seen her between three and four o'clock in the afternoon when he had given her 8d, the daily rate for the room, and asked her to go downstairs and pay the lodging house deputy. The couple had argued earlier and to cheer her up, he also gave her a shilling to do with as she wished. He then returned to bed, his usual routine after finishing work. Working on the markets meant early morning starts which ensured his day generally ended around mid-afternoon. He slept until around 'half past ten or eleven o'clock' that night and when he awoke, she was not in the room, which he said was unusual because she had never been prone to going out much at night. He went downstairs to try and ascertain where she had gone and discovered when she had left, she had not paid the money for the room to the lodging house deputy, Elizabeth Ryder. The two of them discussed it but, Mrs Ryder expressed no real concerns, the room rate could be settled later and so he went back to bed.

As far as he was concerned, at that point all was well. He expected Alice to return, pay the bill and everything would return to normal. Obviously, it did not.

There was little other evidence of note. Elizabeth Ryder confirmed much of what McCormack told the court and added that as far as she was aware Alice had not worked as a prostitute during the time she lived at the house. If anything, according to her testimony, Alice was in bed most nights by ten o'clock.

PC Joseph Allen, whose beat crossed that of PC Andrews, the officer who discovered Alice's body, told the court how he had passed through Castle Alley at around 12.20 a.m., entering from Whitechapel Road. He lingered near to the lamp post for around five minutes whilst he had something to eat before walking on through the alley and out on to Wentworth Street. Once there he and PC Andrews had met briefly, the two exchanging a few words before going their separate ways. He recalled passing the landlord of the Three Crowns, which stood at the end of the alley, as he was locking up the pub for the night which caused him to check his watch. The time, he recalled, was half past midnight.

At around the same time, the wife of who was termed in court as a superannuated constable was checking doors and closing the curtains of her home which overlooked the alley. From her window, she had a clear view across to the lamp post and although she had not seen PC Allen, she knew the time to be around half past midnight. She concurred with the constable that the alley at that time was quiet and there was no noise to indicate movement of any sort. All of which suggested Alice McKenzie had probably entered Castle Alley at some time between 12.30 and 12.45 a.m., the only window of opportunity created by Andrews and Allen as their beats took them in opposite directions – although from which direction Alice entered seems not to have been debated.

PC Walter Andrews, in his later evidence, expanded on his initial police statement as to the position of the body when he first saw it, which gave a potential pointer. He recalled her head lay on the very edge of the kerbstone which separated the pedestrian walkway from the narrow road, her feet pointed towards the building beside her. On that roadway, and hiding her completely from one side of the alleyway, were two wagons, a scavenger's wagon, and a brewer's dray. Her head, as he recalled, lay almost beneath that scavenger wagon with her lower torso stretched out across the walkway. As a result, she would not have been visible from the narrow road housing the various work-a-day vehicles. The blood he remembered, which was still flowing from wounds he saw on the left side of her neck, had pooled around her body. But it was all on the ground, there were no blood splashes or bloody trail leading away from the body and he believed she had been standing beside the lamp post when attacked.

There was a little more corroborating evidence from his sergeant and a constable, George Neve, who was sent out to check pedestrian movement on the surrounding streets, not that he saw any. However, he did contest the earlier evidence from both John McCormack and Elizabeth Ryder. As far as he was concerned, Alice McKenzie had been a regular out on the streets over the past year, generally between ten and eleven o'clock at night and often 'the worse for wear', as he put it, through drink. He told the coroner his belief that Alice McKenzie was a working prostitute – probably not something John McCormack wanted to admit in public, particularly if he had been a beneficiary of her earnings.

Day two of the inquest, at the same location and with the same coroner, examined in more detail the nature of Alice's death and the wounds inflicted. It brought Detective Inspector Edmund Reid to the stand, a familiar face in Wynne Baxter's courtroom, to recount what he observed whilst the body was still in situ. Much of this corroborated PC Andrew's earlier testimony, the exception being that rather than lying on her right when he arrived at the scene she was on her back. As for the wounds to her neck, he only saw one, the other being somewhat obscured by the body's position on the ground and the still-flowing blood. He went on to explain how the search was organised and managed in the area surrounding the murder site. He then spoke of the arrival of Dr Phillips, the fact it had been raining, and also recalled how the lighting in the alley had been poor, despite there being five lamps along its length, not just the one initially reported and beneath which the body had been discovered. He also told the coroner when Alice's body was lifted on to the ambulance cart, a clay pipe, full of tobacco but unsmoked, had been found.

Dr Phillips followed with cursory details of some of his findings of the post-mortem that had been carried out, essentially confirming there were superficial wounds to the abdomen and two significant wounds to the neck. The first was 4 inches long, and 4 inches below the chin so deep it had divided muscle at the back of the neck. The second cut, made below the first, and which he believed had been made from behind, added to his belief that death must have been instantaneous. Little else was put to the court after the medical evidence and so a third adjournment was made with a date for resumption set for August.

Twenty-four hours after that adjournment, a man William Brodie walked into Leman Street police station and confessed to the murder. If believed it would perhaps have solved some of the Ripper murders and changed the way we all now view the events of 1888. But, as with most things 'Jack', nothing is as it seems. William Brodie had a police record. He had been arrested back in 1877 and charged with larceny, which had resulted in a fourteen-year sentence from which he had been released on licence on 22 August 1888. Shortly after his release, he reported in at Leman Street police station to inform them of his intention to sail on the SS *Africana* to South Africa. Nothing else had been heard from him until 16 July 1889 when he turned up again at Leman Street to inform them he had returned. So, clearly he was known to police and seems to have followed the terms of his licence, which were to report his whereabout to the station.

According to his statement, he admitted to a murder carried out 'up a court way off High Street, Whitechapel at about 2 a.m.'. He goes on to confirm his trip to South Africa but not on the SS *Africana*. He was, he states, a third–class passenger on board the SS *Athenian*. Once there, he obtained work in the diamond mines at Kimberley, returning to London on board the SS *Trojan* arriving on Monday, 15 July 1889, two days before the murder and with a background police were easily able to check.

But from that point on, his statement becomes a rambling wreck full of odd, unbelievable facts mixed in with a few truths. He claimed to have visited his brothers on the day before the murder (16 July) then travelled to Cornwall where he stayed only ten minutes before returning; the journey back being faster than the train by about half an hour. He then states he walked around for some three or four hours before going into a square, through an entrance, off Whitechapel Road where he saw costermongers' barrows and hundreds of people. He claimed to have waited until everyone had left. The time, he thought, was '17.21 o'clock'. Then he saw a woman dressed in red, asked her for sex, paid 1 shilling and killed her using a knife he had subsequently left at the public baths on Lambeth Road.

Clearly, a man suffering some sort of mental breakdown, which Inspector Moore acknowledged in a notation at the end of Brodie's signed statement. Nevertheless, he ensured everything in the statement was checked. Investigations revealed the brothers he had alluded to, James and Thomas Brodie, were printers and neither were in Whitechapel, nor had been for several days. In addition, Cornwall had never been on his list of places visited after returning from South Africa because he had turned up at the printing offices on both 16 and 17 July. Furthermore, he could never have been in Castle Alley at the time of the murder because, after discovering where he had been lodging, it transpired he had been found drunk and asleep in the toilet that night and taken up to his bed.

Not that any of this stopped him being charged with the Alice McKenzie murder. On 20 July, he was brought up before Mr Lushington at the magistrates' court. He advised the charge be made based upon the confession, erroneous though it proved to be. As a result, that put Brodie into prison where he was monitored by the prison doctor. On his reappearance in court seven days later, he advised the charge be withdrawn. Brodie, according to his assessment suffered from acute alcoholism causing hallucinations.

Brodie was duly released, immediately re-arrested on a charge of fraud, then sent to King's Cross police station. Two weeks later, the adjourned inquest was re-opened and Brodie, his statement or his involvement was never mentioned. In fact, this final inquest stage heard nothing new regarding Alice's movements on the night of her murder, or about suspects seen or interviewed. There were no suspects so, unlike in the Frances Coles case, there was no pressure on the coroner's jury to return a verdict favourable to a police trial. Much more interesting was further information about the wounds Alice had sustained, and the strange discovery of a second clay pipe. It had been found prior to the autopsy taking place and was amongst Alice's clothing. What was frustrating for the court was that Dr Phillips had to admit that having found the pipe prior to the post-mortem, it had since been broken accidentally and lost; it never appeared in court, or anywhere else for that matter. If true, this pipe, which Dr Phillips said had been used, was in all likelihood Alice McKenzie's, and the one found beneath her body quite possibly that of her killer.

As for the wounds, he elaborated a little more on his earlier evidence and told the court one wound had possibly put her on the ground, the second, delivered whilst she had been on her back, had been inflicted, as he had stated shortly after the body's discovery, by a killer on her right. Wounds to her abdomen were most definitely inflicted after death and the knife used was sharp, short-bladed and pointed.

The profile of a killer? Well in the absence of any confirmatory profile being in existence in 1891 supposition would suggest a man who has killed before, knows how to disable his victim with lightning speed, kills in the same way every time, puts his victim on the floor, delivers the killer thrust from the right and manages to walk away when surrounded by police.

Surely, this killing sequence was mirrored in the murder beneath that archway in Swallow Gardens. If James Sadler did one, could he not have done two? Surely, given the Ripper series of murders, police must have seen the similarities between the killings of Alice McKenzie and Frances Coles.

That does not automatically mean he was a double murderer or that he even had anything to do with either case. But the similarity here is too emphatic to have been ignored. It is likely that the investigation team, which involved policemen who had also been involved in the Castle Alley case, saw the parallels. These two cases, as with a number of the 1888 cases, strongly suggest one hand at work. No doubt that was why the press and several senior police officers felt both were the Ripper in almost every detail. Both, like all the rest, also raised the same question: How did these two women meet their deaths in the midst of a heavy police presence and how come they, let alone their killer, passed by unseen?

PART THREE

QUESTIONS AND SUSPICIONS

Chapter 13

Failure

According to quotes attributed to 'The London correspondent of the *Manchester Evening News*' and published by various newspapers around the time of the third resumed inquest into Frances Coles, the identity of Jack the Ripper, whether in plain sight or not, was known. Not, of course, to the public at large, but to stipendiary magistrate, Montagu Williams, one-time English teacher, army officer, barrister and often quoted in the press because of his keen interest in the Whitechapel murders. A subject he felt eminently qualified to discuss in print in later life, justified he claimed, because he had been told of the real killer's identity.

He was known to both Coroner Wynne Baxter and Chief Inspector Donald Swanson. The latter because of his involvement in the murder trial of Percy Lefroy Mapleton, the railway murderer who was defended by Montagu Williams, Wynne Baxter through his role of Sussex coroner when he presided over the inquest into Lefroy Mapleton's victim, Isaac Gold, at Balcombe in 1881.

Whether that gave more credibility to the story he eventually hinted at in the second of two autobiographical books written about his life, *Later Leaves*, and published at the time of Frances Coles's murder and long, drawn-out inquest, is obviously not known. It seems neither man ever discussed publicly the legal advocate's claim. But if he was right, it did have a relevance, albeit somewhat tenuous, simply because Montagu Williams's claim he had been given the identity of the man responsible for all the Whitechapel murders in 1888 was never going to be made public. He decided, for some ridiculously obscure reason, it was his secret to keep: 'He declines, however, in the most tantalising way to take the reader into his confidence, though he declares that the cessation of the East-end murders dates from the time when certain action was taken as a result of the promulgation of the ideas he alludes to,' was how the press reported it. Meaning, essentially, the Ripper crimes had ended with the death of Mary Jane Kelly and certain practices being implemented by police, which prevented a resumption of his murder spree. What those practices were he never explained. Suffice to say, the killing had stopped and that the identity of this perpetrator, this mass murderer, would likely never now be revealed. Frances Coles's murder, therefore, as far as Montagu Williams was concerned, was not to be added to the Ripper's variable list of victims.

If true, in theory at least, then James Thomas Sadler was never going to be pronounced guilty by the jury that took their place for the final time at The Working Lads' Institute on 27 February 1891. Leastways, not on the basis that he had also murdered a number of women in the summer of 1888. Those earlier crimes, despite continued press speculation, were not to be laid at his doorstep. A conclusion Chief Inspector Swanson and the investigating team had reached days earlier anyway. For them, at this stage of proceedings, and after what had been a relatively short investigation, that past decade of murder had to be set aside. This was a case that revolved around only one event, the murder of Frances Coles. It may be fair to assume there were perhaps some dissenting voices in police ranks, particularly regarding his possible involvement in certain previous unsolved cases, though this coroner's court was not the place to have aired those concerns in public.

At this stage of the inquest procedure, it could only be speculation anyway. They had no historic evidence to link him to anything other than the Frances Coles murder. Probably, were the jury verdict to go their way, other links may well have been sought. But first, they must prove their suspicions in the Swallow Gardens' case and, unfortunately, it was not going well. The witness evidence presented to Wynne Baxter's court from all parties had confused rather than clarified Sadler's supposed guilt. Anomalies to do with time and Sadler's apparent drunkenness were the most obvious key failings. Yet on the plus side, they probably felt they had managed to create some doubt, particularly over Sadler's erratic movements on the night of the murder. They had also proven the link between victim, suspected killer and the weapon used; the latter the investigation's biggest success. The logic is straightforward enough. If Sadler had owned the knife, sold it, then denied doing so, he was guilty. As the jury took their places for what would prove to be the final act, there may have been some optimism amongst Leman Street's police, despite what had gone before; hopeful those three key facts would be enough to swing the verdict in their favour and take James Sadler to the next stage: trial for murder.

Would that have then brought back into focus the murder of Alice McKenzie in 1889? The answer may be yes but there is nothing in police files to suggest it was the case, although it is likely they did revisit the murder file. Sadler may not have fit all the various killer profiles suggested at the time, but he certainly fit one: he was a sailor. Perhaps it was at the back of everyone's mind as they took their seats in that coroner's court. James Sadler and his career at sea, could have operated on the periphery of the Ripper. A second killer if you like, never before countenanced but not so easily dismissed.

Whether Coroner Wynne Baxter ever considered the link is doubtful. In this final stage of a long, drawn-out inquest his duty was clear: understand the movements of the victim and suspect; explain the circumstances of the murder; and if the evidence supported it, suggest a jury verdict naming a killer. To that end, the morning began with further evidence from police. Street plans were shown to the jurors showing the distances between various locations scattered around the Whitechapel area relevant to the murder site.

Inspector Moore explained how the police had handled the enquiry into Frances Coles's death and the circumstances that led to Sadler being charged with 'wilfully causing the death of Frances Coles', on 15 February. He gave details of the search they made of his clothes, what had been found – none of which had been incriminating – and Sadler's response to the charge: 'Yes, yes, yes, yes.'

A low-key response to a serious accusation, possibly because he was trying to grasp the reasoning behind the charge, having just learnt Duncan Campbell had informed police about the knife. 'The old man had made a mistake about the knife. He never saw me,' was Sadler's only recorded comment about Campbell's accusation, duly logged by the inspector. Police records suggest he never made any further statement about the knife's discovery.

Inspector Reid added to Moore's overall picture of events and the investigating procedures followed by the enquiry team and gave a general outline of how enquiries had been conducted. The two men completed police evidence and testimony at an inquest that to all intents and purposes had been a pre-trial hearing.

Coroner Wynne Baxter then heard an account of the early hours of that February morning from Kate McCarthy and Thomas Fowler, the two lovers who made earlier statements to police about what they saw happening on Royal Mint Street, William 'Jumbo' Friday also told again his story of seeing a couple in a doorway. He still held to his belief that one of that couple had been Frances, recognised not by seeing her face but the hat she was wearing. But by this stage of the hearing, his testimony was given little credence. Police had made it clear, since the early stages of their enquiry, they thought he had been mistaken. That left the floor to Sadler's barrister, Mr Lawless.

He called Ellen Calanna, alias Calman.

This was the woman whose earlier statement to police at Leman Street had not, it would seem, received the level of consideration it ought to have demanded. Possibly, as pointed out earlier, because she was deemed unreliable after it became clear the times she had given police initially were found to be inconsistent with the events of the night in question; a view compounded by her later press statement which again contained contradictory evidence when she discussed time and place. Although this was amended on that second visit to the police station, by then she was thought to have been influenced by what she had since heard or been told. Sadler's barrister, a man who had been critical of any and all evidence heard in that coroner's court described as 'time specific', felt differently. Unconcerned about how and when Ellen Calanna met with Frances, the times she had given, vague though they were, still offered up a reasonable account of one isolated event, namely the meeting between the two women and the sailor on Commercial Street, the one key incident on the night of the murder he must have known would have the greatest impact on the jurors sitting in that courtroom. Testimony heard by that stage over Sadler's movements had placed him almost 1 mile away in the dock area.

Whether Ellen Calanna, as she began her evidence, had any notion of the importance her testimony was to have is doubtful. The inquest had been running for two weeks. There had been a huge amount of testimony heard over the five sessions, from fifty-five witnesses, and much of it unreported in the press. So, unless street gossip had kept her up to date, she would have had little idea how influential her own version of events on the night Frances died would be. Besides, this was not a criminal trial, despite how it probably felt to Sadler and the importance it held for the police case. Nevertheless, it must have been daunting for Calanna to give her evidence, a woman who must have thought after her two visits to Leman Street police she had been disparaged and disbelieved because of her station in life. A street prostitute, an 'unfortunate' woman, as society viewed her at that time, living in one of the poorest areas of London. But for Mr Lawless, who had summoned her to court, and indirectly to James Thomas Sadler, she was at that moment the most important woman in the capital. She, more than any other in the room that day, understood why Frances Coles had spent a large chunk of her adult life enduring the same grinding existence as herself.

Their association, she told Wynne Baxter, went back five years to their first meeting back in 1886. Frances was a familiar face on the streets around Whitechapel. So were a number of the men she associated with, spent time in pubs with and who, on occasion, paid her for sexual favours. Amongst that group was a man whose face she knew, James Sadler – important because on the night Frances was murdered, Ellen was able to tell the jury what perhaps they already suspected. The sailor who approached the two of them when they stood on Commercial Street – the man wearing the cheese-cutter hat and the shiny boots, the man who assaulted her and lured Frances away with the half-crown – she had never seen before. He was a stranger, someone new to her part of Whitechapel and without a shadow of a doubt, not James Sadler.

Here was the defining moment in the Frances Coles inquest. From the moment Ellen Calanna said those words, the jurors could not find Sadler guilty. The hiring of Mr H. H. Lawless had been a priceless decision. If Frances Coles had been seen walking off towards the Minories, which put her in the vicinity of Swallow Gardens, with a sailor in shiny boots at around 2 a.m. then, as far as most were concerned, that man was her killer. He was also the elusive Jack the Ripper.

Coroner Wynne Baxter appeared to share the same view when he addressed the jury at the conclusion of the inquest. In a lengthy summing up, he reviewed the evidence that had been presented, splitting it, according to press reports, into two distinct areas: one that supported the theory Sadler was the man responsible for Frances Coles's death, the other that supported the notion he was not, which included Calanna's testimony. The telling factor as far as Wynne Baxter was concerned, was if the medical men's assessment of the wounds and the manner in which they had been inflicted were correct then it was unlikely that Sadler, who was believed drunk at the vital time, could have inflicted them. The jury agreed. It took only thirteen minutes for them to return a verdict of 'wilful murder against some person or persons unknown', adding they thought police had acted correctly in detaining James Thomas Sadler. The coroner appears to have supported the verdict and added to his earlier assessment of the evidence: 'How the murderer could have eluded the police and railway men was a mystery common to this and similar crimes that preceded it.'

In essence, he seemed to agree with the popular belief that Frances Coles was another Ripper victim and, just as with all the others, the killer had simply vanished when virtually surrounded by police.

The verdict was a disaster for Swanson and his team, who from the outset had stuck rigidly to the belief their murderer was the man they still had in custody, James Sadler. There was also a level of scepticism aimed at Ellen Calanna's testimony, which they believed contributed significantly to the acquittal verdict. In fact, Inspector Moore stated four days later that her evidence in part was untrue: 'Evidence given before the Coroner by Ellen Calanna, alias Calman is untrue, especially with regard to the assault upon her which resulted in her receiving a black eye. Special report submitted.'

The special report appears to have been lost over time so there is no way of knowing what the inspector knew about the events she had talked of, or the veracity of what she had said, although he did not appear to doubt the gist of her story with regard to meeting with Frances nor the times, despite them being less than accurate.

Presumably, what he disagreed with, though never said, were not the words used but what those words had implied. Certainly, Ellen Calanna's testimony did not lead to any shift in police opinion when it came to Frances Coles's killer. Enough circumstantial evidence existed to support their theory that despite the coroner's court verdict, the finger of guilt was still firmly pointing at James Sadler and with some justification.

In a report dated 3 March, after a request made by the chief constable, the results of enquiries in Whitechapel revealed that Sadler had stayed at the Victoria Lodging House between 16 and 20 July 1889, the crucial dates around the murder of Alice McKenzie. William Dann, the lodging housekeeper confirmed that Sadler booked himself in after leaving the SS *Bilbao* on 7 July that year. Frances Coles, during this same period, had been lodging at 18 Thrawl Street. Sadler's statement suggested he and Frances had met during that time, but the implication was also that Sadler could have met Alice McKenzie during that same week. Unfortunately, enquiries had failed to establish any such meeting or any sort of connection between the two women. This is important only because had there been any, no matter how tenuous, it could have linked Sadler to Alice's murder. It seems almost certain the two women had known each other; perhaps not as close friends, but by sight. They drank in the same pubs, they walked the same streets, and no doubt met the same men. It would, therefore, have been difficult not to have at least been acquainted with each other in some manner.

If it had been proven Sadler had committed the murder beneath Arch 45 then the previous similar crime committed in Castle Alley had to be deserving of closer examination. Whether any in-depth work was done in that regard is not known; there are no known files relating to such an investigation. But clearly there was an evolving theory developing back in 1891 and after the Frances Coles inquest verdict, that notion had merit.

Chapter 14

Mylett, Smith and Millwood

The disappointment of the verdict and its ramifications for the police case against Sadler were plain to see to all involved in the investigation. Whatever police deliberations took place after the jury's pronouncement would have been affected by what was effectively a not guilty verdict against the man they were still holding in the cells. It meant there was a decision to be made. James Sadler's next public appearance would be before Mr Mead in the police court. If the inquest verdict had supported the police investigation, they would now be setting out their case for trial. As things were, after the coroner's pronouncement, there was no charge on which to prosecute further without there being a significant improvement in the quality of the evidence presented. As the inquest jury had effectively declared him innocent, it was highly unlikely the police court would do otherwise. For Charles Mathews that meant unless something new was forthcoming, the case against James Thomas Sadler was closed.

If there were any suspicions lurking in the background linking Sadler to any previous murder cases surely this was the time to explore them. As suggested earlier, the question of his possible culpability in certain unsolved cases from the previous decade must have arisen. Alice McKenzie aside, which was probably re-examined, along with the five canonical Ripper murders, in which he could have played no part, were there any others? Today there is a tendency to view all murders in that infamous period as being the work of one man. But did Whitechapel's police view it the same way? Life in that district of London in the later part of the nineteenth century was fraught with danger. There had been ten confirmed, unsolved murders between 1888 and 1891. To make matters worse, it was extremely difficult to tie all these killings together. The common factor, with only one exception, the murder of Mary Kelly, was that these murders had taken place on the streets around Whitechapel. The killer, or killers, had operated out in the open in the early hours of the morning. One victim had been stabbed to death, one had been strangled, seven had their throats cut and four of them had also been mutilated. Establishing any patterns was clearly difficult. Popular belief, as discussed earlier, was that the killer could be a sailor, a man who had an easy means of escape and could ensure he was never around the Whitechapel area once police enquiries began.

This viewpoint, as has already been stated, was not without merit or support and, of course, James Sadler fitted aspects of that killer profile. As police had uncovered in the Frances Coles case alone, he clearly had a seagoing history that stretched back into the 1870s; he came from a family where the sea had been an integral part of past family life and was more than familiar with how the street life of Whitechapel operated. He had a full grasp of how local life functioned on a daily basis; which prostitutes worked in certain areas (and how), the public houses they used and the lodging houses they stayed in.

None of this would have been lost on the police operating out of Leman Street. They would not have needed much persuasion to point a finger in the general direction of men sharing Sadler's occupation. The place was full of sailors every day, but how many were killers? Statistically, not many, which is what made him so interesting. James Sadler, innocent or guilty, had put himself into a precarious position through his relationship with Frances. He had also created doubt as to his innocence when he put together a deliberately vague statement twenty-four hours or so after her murder. When he sat down in front of Chief Inspector Donald Swanson, a man well versed in obfuscation, he was sober. The notion that he could not remember salient, relevant points, untrue. He was a dissembler, being economical with the truth and creating a false timeline around the events of the night of Frances Coles's death. That does not necessarily mean he acted in that way over guilt. Involvement with the police on any level could have been a sufficient catalyst to confuse and mislead, though it does raise a reasonable suspicion that personal guilt had played a part.

The question of his involvement in other murders, therefore, has to be valid and it is likely that Swanson and his group of detectives took it seriously, though that in itself posed its own difficulties. Moving away from what are deemed the main Ripper murders there is little else Sadler could have been involved in. Whitechapel, over the years before and after those murders, had seen various amounts of violence inflicted on women late at night, fed generally by alcohol consumed in too great a quantity and too late into the night. But murder, despite the apparently high body count, was not generally that common. Other than Alice McKenzie, there was only Martha Tabram, back in early August 1888, when Sadler was known to have still been living with his wife, and the later murders of Rose Mylett and Emma Smith as possible victims.

The Mylett case had raised some press interest after she was discovered on 20 December 1888 in a place known as Clarke's Yard, High Street, Poplar. But it was not the level of fevered press reporting that followed the discovery of Frances Coles three years later, possibly because her death had not followed the pattern of previous killings. Here there was no blood, no knife attack, no obvious Ripper-style killing. Mylett, who like many other Whitechapel prostitutes used various aliases, Millett and Davies being two of them, was found at 4.15 a.m. that December morning. Bow Division's Police Sergeant Robert Golding, discovered her body lying on her left side just inside the narrow entrance into the yard and, according to his later report, her body was still warm, her clothes appeared not to have been disarranged, she wore no hat and there were no signs of a struggle. His brief, cursory examination found no blood, no visible wounds, and no obvious signs of murder. After a more extensive examination carried out by Dr George Harris, who attended the scene in place of divisional surgeon, Matthew Brownfield, concurred with the sergeant's initial opinion and her body was removed to the mortuary.

At that stage, there were no suspicious circumstances surrounding the death and no alarm had been raised by the police, though it is fair to say they were cautious. This was a dead woman found some six weeks after the appalling horror that the Ripper had wrought on Mary Jane Kelly at Miller's Court, which meant that an automatic, if initially low key, criminal enquiry into the death began within minutes of the discovery. What police did not appear to do was make any rash judgements or instantly raise its profile amongst their own officers or the press. In fact, all reporting by local newspapers regarding the discovery was, strangely enough, kept to a minimum – somewhat unusual for a media outlet that produced lurid articles on every aspect of every Whitechapel murder case throughout the summer of that year. No doubt because at that early stage, the police, in the absence of any obvious cause of death, decided they had no reason to declare this a murder, let alone point a finger at the Ripper as its perpetrator.

Their decision was shown to be premature after mortuary attendant, Thomas Chivers, during his routine examination of the body, claimed to have seen a mark around the neck indicative of strangulation. Bow Division police surgeon, Matthew Brownfield, who carried out the initial post-mortem the following day, agreed. Rose Mylett, according to his later testimony to the coroner, had died as a result of being strangled by what he described as 'a four-fold cord', which had been drawn from the right side of her spine to the back of the left ear lobe. He also found impressions made by her thumbs and middle and index fingers on each side of her neck, caused in all probability by her attempt to stop the strangulation. He found no other signs of a struggle.

Knowledge of that discovery found its way to newly appointed police commissioner, James Monro. Concerned he could become embroiled in yet another Ripper murder, he alerted the Metropolitan Police's divisional surgeon-in-chief, Dr Alexander MacKellar. That intervention resulted in a second post-mortem some days later which, perhaps unexpectedly, reinforced Brownfield's prognosis and was later supported by H Division's Dr Phillips. Rose Mylett's death, according to these expert medical men, had indeed been caused by strangulation.

These conclusions changed the complexion of the police investigation, but not in the same way as if the killing had been categorised as a Ripper murder. The findings of the doctors were, in some quarters at least, seen as contentious. Sergeant Golding, first policeman on the scene, is reported to have held the opinion she had died as a result of falling whilst drunk, and asphyxiated on the stiff collar of her own dress, a view apparently shared by others in the medical world. Differing perspectives which muddied the waters somewhat and ensured the police investigation into the death became stunted. Too many variable, complex and conflicting views about the manner of her death possibly meant the investigation never established a clear direction to follow.

Neither did it fall to police at Leman Street to mount, or be a part of the overall investigation. That fell to Detective Inspector Wilding, chief detective at Bow police station. A man who, initially at least, seemed to take the view that if it was murder, and a continuation of the Ripper killings then police manpower needed to facilitate a comprehensive enquiry had to be increased. Whether or not it was is doubtful, given the confusion over how she had died. What it perhaps did was focus the mind and centre enquiries more around Rose Mylett's true identity and background than how she had died.

According to newspaper reports, she was 26 years old, born in Ireland, and had only 1s 2d in her dress pocket when found. Local police believed her to have worked as a prostitute whilst living at 18 George Street, Spitalfields. The formal identity, made by a woman named Elizabeth Usher, also revealed she had been an inmate of Bromley Sick Asylum during the first three months of 1888, a hospital for the sick and poor that was kept separate from the workhouse. Alice Groves, with whom she had shared the lodging house, told police that on the night of the murder, Rose had borrowed 2d from the lodging house landlady, Mrs Smith, to pay for a tram fare. Just where she went Alice claimed not to know but did tell police she had seen Rose at about 2.30 a.m. that same morning, drunk, in the company of two sailors and walking along Commercial Road.

This sighting was quickly confirmed by a young woman named Neos Green, who lived in High Street, Poplar. According to the *Oxfordshire Weekly News*, which ran the story, another young woman who had also seen these sailors, though much later in the night and not with Rose, but close to Clarke's Yard and in a definite hurry. They were trying to find their way to the West India Dock and had asked her for directions.

By the time Coroner Wynne Baxter opened the delayed inquest into Rose Mylett's possible murder, police had a reasonable picture of who she was, where she had been and her lifestyle. They also believed her work as a prostitute was responsible for how and why she had found her way into Clarke's Yard minutes before her death. According to various press reports this was not something easily accomplished. The yard itself was secured by two high wooden doors or gates, kept shut at night and the only possible access was through the rear where there was a narrow opening. Local beat officer, Thomas Costello, whose responsibility was to check the gate security and patrol the general area, told the coroner he had been past the exact spot where her body was found six times that night. According to his evidence, the night had been clear and he had not seen the sailors mentioned by Neos Green.

There was no other evidence of note and other than the brief sighting on Commercial Road, no one else had come forward with confirming testimony of Rose's movements in the hours leading up to her death. What was heard in the coroner's court, was confirmation of her drinking habits, her wayward street life, and her admittance into the sick asylum shortly after the start of the new year. Hers had been 'a fast life', according to one witness. Ultimately, of course, that same life may well have put her into harm's way.

If Dr Matthew Brownfield's reprise of his earlier autopsy report was to be believed, then it had. For Wynne Baxter, who had no doubt officiated over inquests in the past where strangulation had featured heavily in medical evidence, it needed further clarification. Strangulation, as he knew well enough, could be carried out in various ways. To aid both his court and the ongoing police investigation he wanted the doctor to be more forthcoming. At this stage of the enquiry into Rose Mylett's death, he was well aware of the differing opinions surrounding the case. What he sought was clarity. Experience perhaps had taught him that in such cases, when given latitude to do so doctors were capable of far greater elucidation than they often exhibited outside of his court. Brownfield was no exception. After being asked to interpret the marks found on the victim's neck for the court, he readily did so, explaining to the jury how, in his medical opinion, her killer must have stood behind her and on her left side and then thrown a cord around her neck, pulled it tight, crossing his hands as he did so, which explained the lack of marks at the back of the neck. The use of two rings or holes, as he described it, through which the rope had passed gave traction as he then twisted it by the turning of the wrist until she was dead.

For Wynne Baxter and his jury, that testimony could have left no doubt. Whatever misgivings others outside of his courtroom may have had, for the coroner there was none. Rose Mylett had met her death at the hands of a murderer, a man, it would seem, who simply wanted nothing from his victim other than her life. The murder profile differed to that of the Whitechapel killer of a couple of months earlier only because there was no knife involved. But, according to modern thinking, killers evolve. So, an argument the Ripper had done exactly that and struck again has merit. Mutilation happened only if there was time to carry it out and Wynne Baxter's jury seemed to agree. They needed little time to debate the pros and cons and were easily swayed into returning a verdict of murder. It ought to have been enough to stir the police into more action. Unfortunately, it did not. The confusion caused by diverse opinions, which did not support the jury verdict and in turn negated any notion of the Ripper's return, won the day, and the Rose Mylett murder case was quietly shelved without even the manner of her death being resolved.

How does this fit with James Sadler? Well, he was on shore at the time. He left the SS *Winestead* on 1 October that year and did not go back to sea until the new year. The link is tenuous but, unlike countless other suspects, he should not simply be ruled out. He also has to be looked at closely in relation to the murder of 45-year-old Emma Smith. She had been murdered in April 1888, nine months before Rose Mylett. The two women had lived at the same lodging house. Whether they lived in the lodgings at the same time or knew each other is not known, but it cannot be beyond the realms of possibility. Emma was known to have lived there for around eighteen months prior to her death. According to her story, she had been attacked by two or three men in Osborne Street, some 300 yards away from her lodgings. She survived the attack but later died in hospital from peritonitis and although not murdered in the same way as the later Ripper victims, was recorded by many as being his first. There was no knife involved here. Emma died as a result of a blunt object being thrust into her vagina; the resultant internal injuries and infection causing her death. But it must be remembered that reference is always made to the Whitechapel murders as being committed by one man, because by association the killer is always labelled Jack the Ripper, a brand name probably invented by a newspaper man looking for a headline. However, it does not automatically follow that one man carried out all the attacks around that district from 1888 to 1891. There is room for another and the man that murdered Emma Smith, Rose Mylett, Alice McKenzie and Frances Coles could well be a second 'Jack the Ripper'.

There are also the women who were attacked and escaped, such as Ada Wilson, mentioned in Paul Begg's excellent book, *Jack the Ripper: The Facts.* She was stabbed twice in the throat whilst in her home at Bow, not far from the East India dock, in March 1888 and recovered from appalling injuries. The attacker, again possibly a sailor, was never caught.

Then there is the rarely written about 38-year-old Annie Millwood who had been living at 8 White's Row, Whitechapel. Another stabbing victim, she was attacked in late February 1888, and admitted to the Whitechapel Infirmary. According to newspaper reports, she had been stabbed in the legs and lower part of her body by a man wielding a clasp knife. Annie was critically ill for weeks afterwards but eventually rallied and made a full recovery. Released in late March, she was taken in by the South Grove Workhouse on Mile End Road where she stayed until early April. Unfortunately for her it was not to be the start of a new life. She collapsed and died in the early part of that month, though the cause of her death was not thought to be connected to the earlier attack. Similarities also exist between her attack and one perpetrated upon Martha Tabram, another lodger from a house on George Street. She was murdered on 7 August 1888; her body discovered at around 5 a.m., stabbed thirty-nine times – the wounds spread across the chest, abdomen and vagina. Again, possibly by a different killer but linked to Jack the Ripper simply because of the women's association with Whitechapel.

Although James Sadler was never implicated in any of these earlier killings or attacks, as far as is known, throughout the first eight months of 1888 he was living with his wife at various addresses in Whitechapel. Police enquiries after his arrest for the Frances Coles murder, and his wife's subsequent interview with Donald Swanson, revealed he had been residing at 14 Thomas Street, Commercial Road in the early part of the year, and had moved to Johnson Street (or Yard) by spring/summer. There were no doubt other addresses to add but, given the transient nature of Whitechapel's workforce and poorly maintained rental records, these were never verified.

That interview between Sarah Sadler and the inspector, like the one between her husband and the police at Leman Street, had been sparse on detail. Whatever information she had given was vague and not necessarily accurate either when it came to how, when, and to where, she and James had moved home. This seems to have been the norm, as with many others in Whitechapel around that time. Work in 1880s Whitechapel was poorly paid, and for some, hard to get. Moving addresses was dictated by circumstances brought on by lack of income. But it did mean the Sadlers were living within the area of these earlier attacks and killings. A retrospective view would perhaps look less favourably on him today than back in 1891 after the Frances Coles murder. Being a 'living close by', resident certainly creates suspicion. Obviously, this is speculation, but between 1887 and the summer of 1888 he was holding down a job on land, maybe not being paid on a regular basis, but generally in good financial health with the family income coming solely, as far as is known, from labouring in warehouses in Cutler Street, Houndsditch, or general dock work. History also shows he liked to drink and had exhibited a violent streak in his own marriage.

So, when it came to making that decision as to whether or not to continue pressing the case against him regardless of the verdict in the coroner's court there could well have been an argument in favour. There seems little doubt police still believed him guilty; no other suspects were under investigation according to files still in existence, and no search was ever mounted to find Ellen Calanna's man in shiny boots. But, as far as is known, neither did they search for tangible evidence to link Sadler to any of these earlier murders no matter how tenuous. All of which meant unless new evidence emerged to connect Sadler with any unsolved case, Frances Coles included, there was little point in proceeding further.

On 2 March, presumably after lengthy discussions amongst officers at Leman Street police station, that inevitable decision was communicated to Messrs Wilson and Wallis, James Sadler's solicitors, by letter:

Immediate. – Solicitors Department, Treasury, 2nd March, 1891.
Dear Sirs, – Re Sadler. So far as the prosecution is concerned it is not Intended to offer evidence to-morrow before the magistrate therein, And application will be made to him to permit the adoption of this course.
Faithfully yours (signed) T. CUFFE
21 Bow Street, W.C.

For James Sadler, of course, it meant instant freedom and for the thousands that had gathered outside to witness his release, it rectified a wrong. According to Inspector Moore in his later report, Sadler was taken away from court in a cab by his solicitor and a representative of *The Star* newspaper. It was believed they had agreed to pay for Sadler's story and were thought to have contributed to his defence. No doubt for the inspector and the officers at Leman Street police station, it must have been a blow and the short paragraph he adds at the end of that report sums up the police position at that time: 'No persons have been detained in this Division during the day in connection with this case.'

He could have added, nor ever will be!

Chapter 15

Aftermath

A footnote with a relevance for the following decade and beyond. As already shown, as far as police were concerned James Thomas Sadler had killed Frances Coles. For others coming later to this particular crime, there is the question, 'What about Jack the Ripper?' If Sadler did not do it, who did? Based on the weapon used, the victim's position in Whitechapel's poor society, the nature of the wounds inflicted and location of the attack, why could it not have marked a return to the dark days of 1888? The collapse of Sadler's intended prosecution meant that, along with all those murders preceding it, the case would never be closed and forever linked to the shadowy figure that had terrorised the East End of London. For Sadler, who had protested his innocence throughout, it marked a change in life. He left the sea.

During the three weeks following the coroner's court verdict and the collapse of the police case, he disappeared. But his involvement in Frances Coles's murder, albeit by association and not conviction, did not. Throughout his incarceration, there had been fierce speculation as to his guilt. In some quarters unfairly, a number of newspapers had taken, let's say, a more biased view as to his involvement in the killing. Sadler himself felt his position in everyday society had been damaged severely by the publication of that newspaper interview with his estranged wife. He wanted recompense. Two days after walking away from the police court a free man, London's *Globe* newspaper published the following short paragraph:

> Wilson and Wallis solicitors to James Sadler issued a statement saying they had been instructed by James Sadler to take action against a number of newspapers for the publication of statements alleged to be libellous in connecting their client with the recent murder in Swallow Gardens.

It was payback time. The funding for this action has never been clearly identified. Sadler had no money when he took his place in that cab outside the court and none was forthcoming. So, presumably, the funds had come from *The Star* newspaper or the Seamen's Union. Either way, in the short term at least, it offered little by way of financial reward at a time when James Sadler really needed it. He was unwell at the start of March, unsurprising given the ordeal he had just gone through, and travel from prison to court in a draughty, cold, black maria had taken its toll. When the *East London Observer* newspaper tracked him down on 28 March, he was bedridden suffering from bronchitis, but not to such a degree he could not still seize the opportunity to grab a headline.

SADLER
He is found ill and Poverty Stricken In a Shadwell Coffee House

A few words that caught the eye, as the newspaper intended it to. But from the content that followed it was clear Sadler had fallen on hard times. Shadwell, not the best place in London to be living at that time, suffered from widespread opium use, poor, badly sanitised housing, and prostitution at an alarming level. Even the *Globe's* reporter had turned up with a bodyguard and described the coffee house, above which Sadler was living, as being in 'one of the dirtiest and dingiest parts of Shadwell' he had seen. Something Sadler was all too well aware of, but not in a position to do anything about. 'Beggars couldn't be choosers', was how he put it when the two men met in the coffee house's upstairs room. Too ill to leave his bed, the interview was conducted by candlelight in a wide room containing three other beds, all unoccupied, and a single washstand. Sadler's bed was well placed to see out on to the street below.

Ravaged by illness but still keen to talk, Sadler, described by the reporter as a man whose features were set off by 'heavy eyebrows and a thick, dark brown beard', explained his escape to Shadwell as intentional. There had, he claimed, been too much publicity surrounding his appearances at the inquest and he had needed a period of anonymity. How much truth there was in that statement is debatable; had he had the money perhaps he would have hidden himself away elsewhere – not that it would have guaranteed his disappearance remained undisclosed. This reporter had managed to find him and doubtless others would have too, eventually. Police would also have had a continued interest in his whereabouts, as would his wife, despite the two of them being estranged. Besides which, if he won his case against the newspapers, as his solicitors had no doubt suggested he probably would, publicity would have become a friend, something the man from the *Globe* was probably all too well aware of, though not enough to explore it in any great detail. The reporter's main interest lay in encouraging Sadler to talk about the unproven case against him; that was the story he had travelled to Shadwell to find, and Sadler was all too willing to oblige. He started with the account of the knife Duncan Campbell had claimed to have purchased from him for a shilling and a little bit of tobacco. As far as he was concerned, the whole thing had been a set-up. Campbell, he claimed, 'was in the pay of the police'. There had never been a knife.

According to the story he related, subsequently published by the newspaper, everything began with the robbery in Thrawl Street. Frances, as he stated in his original police statement, had stood back when he had been attacked and to his mind at the time, that had been both unhelpful and suspicious. Thrawl Street was her turf, she had lodged there, knew the area and the dangers and he felt justified in being angry. But, he told the reporter, she tried to explain why she had left him to face the attackers alone: 'How could I Jim? You know if I'd lifted as much as a finger for you, I should have been marked by these people and they'd pay me out when they got the opportunity.'

There is perhaps some truth in that. Certainly, Sadler thought so and said he could see some merit in her answer. But that attack, he claimed, had set in motion most of the events of that night. The robbery had taken all his money, which in turn meant he could not afford a bed for the night and forced his return to the docks. In turn, that had led to the fight by the dock gates and his being stopped on the street by a police constable because of the injuries he had sustained. The officer had tried to help and in the course of checking out his injuries, he had also searched him. 'He felt all over my pockets and even down to my sea boots,' then told him to go to hospital and get the wounds looked at. The search, Sadler insisted, proved he had not been carrying a knife prior to the murder.

So, as far as Sadler was concerned in the telling of his story, he and Duncan Campbell had never met. There would have been no point. There was no knife to sell. He had only ever seen Campbell once and that had been at Leman Street police station after he had been placed into an identity parade and the man had been brought into the room to try and pick him out. Something, he insisted, he had failed to do after walking up and down the line-up twice. 'Goodness knows he might have easily enough picked me out for I was wearing my cap at the time, which was all covered and clotted with blood, and my eyes were all swollen and bruised.'

It was a point he also complained about directly to Inspector Moore after the police court released him. Something he and the inspector apparently discussed at length. But the inspector had persuaded him it would not have been in his best interests to pursue.

'You'd better not. You weren't taken to the central criminal court. If you were and Campbell had repeated his evidence there, you might have had ground, but I don't think you'd better take proceedings now ...' was how Sadler quoted the inspector's assessment of his threat to sue. Maybe that's why he had been persuaded to go after the newspapers. Campbell was a harder nut to crack, the press a little easier. After all, they had run with his wife's 'false, lying, and scandalous', story. Though, as he explained when asked about the rationale behind his decision, he thought the *Daily Telegraph* was more culpable than many of the other newspapers. It, he felt, had to bear a greater burden than the rest. The case against the paper, set to be heard in court in early April, would be the deciding factor in his bid against at least 'six others'. Win that, win them all, seemed to be his view at that time.

An understandable sentiment if *The Star*, as was suspected, was footing the legal bill. Sadly though, none of that would detract from the notoriety he had gained through becoming enmeshed in Frances Coles's murder; a burden he would have to carry for the rest of his life. What would not encumber him, however, was the infamy any attachment to the Ripper would have brought. That, as he told the reporter, could no longer be laid at his door, despite anything that had been written to the contrary. The sea and his involvement with it had provided the alibi, should it ever have been needed, to show he was nowhere near London on those crucial dates in 1888.

With nothing else to add, the newspaper man departed, satisfied with his story and James Sadler sank back into obscurity. At least as far as the press and public were concerned. After the interview had been published in the *Globe*, there was no interest in pursuing him further. Even his attempt at extracting compensation from the press, the mechanics of which were already in motion, attracted no further news interest. Neither did continued reportage on the murder itself carry any news value. Like all those earlier cases that were destined to be filed, 'unsolved', its significance was diminished by time. Its investigative value offered little interest to both police and researchers due to the uncertainty surrounding its relevance to what fascinated them more: the presumed Ripper murders of three years earlier. James Thomas Sadler, the main and only suspect in the case, was left behind by time. Just another footnote in the Whitechapel murders story.

Or was he?

Chapter 16

Uncertainty

As far as police were concerned, he was not so easily dismissed; he was still their number one suspect, despite his release due to the lack of supporting evidence. That helped maintain a level of interest in his whereabouts. Had Sadler chosen a quiet life, that interest would no doubt have waned over time, even though there were never any other candidates put forward to replace him at the top of the wanted list. Unfortunately, Sadler had a side to his character, possibly not explored enough after the Swallow Gardens' murder, which was both troublesome and at times unmanageable. He had a violent streak. Over the next three years it surfaced more than once and ensured, despite his best intentions, that he never left the top of that list.

It ought to have been very different. After that interview with the *Globe,* life for James Sadler had improved significantly. The libel cases against the media seem to have gone in his favour. In early May 1891, he came into money and invested in a retail business at 121, Danbrook Road, Lower Streatham. By the middle of that month, perhaps to offset costs, he also took in a lodger, a retired naval pensioner named James Moffatt. By the month's end his wife, Sarah, had also agreed to return and help build both business and home. Throughout the summer of 1891, the business, operating as a chandler's, did well. Sadler's decision to move into retail proved to be a sound one. But as winter swept in, whilst takings at the shop had improved, the relationship with his wife had begun to deteriorate. So much so, and perhaps persuaded by the lodger, Moffatt, she wrote to Chief Inspector Swanson detailing the abuse she was suffering.

The letter led to a meeting between the two of them on 11 December where she described in greater detail the level of violence – though much of it was mental rather than physical abuse. Swanson, ever meticulous, recorded the conversation in a written report, obviously keen to ensure there was a record should the situation between the two of them deteriorate further. Escalation was something Sarah apparently feared most, particularly as Sadler, she claimed, had threatened her life. According to Swanson's report, which is scant on detail, he seems to have had no hesitation in accepting her story was true; he recorded the receipt of her letter and the organising of a meeting in response to her request for help. But help in a specific way. She was not looking for police to restrain or remove Sadler, what she needed more than anything else was guidance as to how to handle what she saw as a developing verbal and violent situation. As Swanson recorded, the object of the letter and her call was to ask advice, for Sadler had not only assaulted her and otherwise treated her cruelly, but he had repeatedly threatened to take her life and she was afraid to live with him any longer.

She believed his attitude had changed towards her since she had moved in because he felt she had not helped enough in the shop. True or not, as Swanson knew all too well, that did not justify Sadler's actions. He advised Sarah to apply to a magistrate, laying out the facts for him to see, and apply for a summons against her husband, which in realty was the only course of action available to her at the time. He also pointed out it would be up to her to decide whether staying together as a couple was still a viable option or not. Other than that, the law on domestic and verbal abuse at that time being clearly inadequate, there was little else he could have done. But after the meeting, he sent a telegram to H Division advising them of Sadler's sudden re-emergence. It is hardly surprising that his suspicions were perhaps reawakened.

Certainly, Chief Inspector Swanson took the threats Sarah Sadler had talked of extremely seriously. Whatever his feelings for James Sadler, he wanted to ensure Sarah remained safe and unharmed. To that end, Streatham police were instructed to monitor the situation at 121 Danbrook Road, which resulted in Police Sergeant Francis Boswell paying a discreet visit five days later. In his follow-up report, he made it clear there had been no further escalation of violence in the household:

> Mrs Sadler, informed me that her husband has not been guilty of any act of violence towards her, or threatened her since she made the complaint to Chief Inspector Swanson on the 10th. Both Mrs Sadler and Moffatt agree in describing Sadler as a most violent, subtle, and treacherous man, in the habit of using the most vile and disgusting language. Mrs Sadler has not applied to the Magistrate for process against her husband at present but states that she shall do so should he use any further violence or threats towards her.

As a result of that visit, which was designed to reassure Sarah Sadler her husband was firmly back on the police's radar, Boswell, after reporting the new situation to senior officers, was instructed to widen the scope of local street patrols in the area. This ensured there was an increased and more visible street presence and was probably standard police practice. It may also have been that they wanted Sadler to know, should he have harboured any lingering doubts, he was being watched. Their strategy may have been less than subtle, but with Christmas approaching and all the stresses it brought with it, for Sarah, that patrolling constable was a daily reassurance. It also proved effective, and the remainder of December passed by peacefully enough.

But as an experienced police officer, Sergeant Boswell was all too well aware that how things looked from the outside was not always reflected by what was happening on the inside. He paid another discreet visit on 1 January 1892 to check. He need not have worried. It seemed Christmas had been good to the Sadlers. He reported things were calm, probably because business had been steadily rising throughout the month. The shop had averaged a daily takings figure of £2 10s, equivalent today of around £205 or just over £1,000 a week. So, as the new year commenced, prospects in the chandlery business were decidedly positive.

But, of course, it did not last. On 4 March 1892, the time noted by Sergeant Boswell as 6.50 p.m., James Moffatt walked into Streatham police station, agitated and upset. He told the sergeant Sadler now refused to allow his wife to leave the house. If she did, according to the elderly pensioner, he would lock her out or assault her. It seemed that since the Christmas period when tempers in the household were less frayed, equanimity had been replaced with rancour and bitterness on Sadler's part. At least, as far as Moffatt was concerned. It seemed the man's actions and general behaviour had suddenly become more irrational than they were at the start of winter.

Boswell obviously sympathised with the old sailor and possibly felt frustrated by Sarah Sadler's failure to heed Chief Inspector Swanson's earlier advice. But presented with the same dilemma and without any other legal option available to him, he could only offer the same recommendation: 'I promised him that attention should be paid by police and advised him to tell Mrs Sadler that the best plan for her to adopt would be to seek advice of the Magistrate at Lambeth Police Court.'

Though he probably thought it a forlorn hope – easier to advise than to do – which Boswell was probably all too aware of. For Sarah Sadler, caught inside an abusive relationship with nowhere else to go, following that advice was possibly fraught with more danger than simply staying where she was. But there was little else Boswell could offer by way of assistance other than make the officers patrolling outside Sadler's property aware of the escalating situation. However, whether to salve his own conscience or simply by way of reassurance, he paid the shop a visit six days later. What he found satisfied him there had been no return to the physical abuse Sarah had complained of back in December. It maybe also reinforced his personal, unspoken view, that Sadler's relationship with his wife had passed the point of no return.

He probably knew from experience that what had happened in the Sadler household was unlikely to rectify itself and there would almost certainly be a tipping point in the months to come. A trigger point perhaps where, despite her reservations, Sarah Sadler would be forced to heed the advice she had steadfastly refused to follow, and of course he was right.

On 9 May, some five or so weeks later, Sarah Sadler walked into Streatham police station after a violent altercation in the early hours of the morning. According to Sergeant Boswell's later report, her husband had threatened again to kill her: 'I beg to report that Mrs Sarah Sadler the wife of James Sadler ... called on me at Streatham Station at 1.15 a.m. 9th inst. And stated that her husband had threatened to cut her throat.'

This time it marked a significant escalation. Threatening to kill her was one thing, threatening to do it in a manner that had put him in the cells just over a year earlier was more than noteworthy. Boswell needed little by way of persuasion this time around to convince her that only a court could now solve her situation. She finally agreed. She and Boswell went in front of magistrate, Mr Hopkins, and within hours he issued a summons for threats.

James Thomas Sadler was back in front of a judge five days later. The hearing was short. He heard evidence presented from his wife and he was bound over 'in his own recognisance of £10 to keep the peace for six months'. From that point on, the marriage was doomed, though it did not, of itself, suffer an instant break-up. Sadler and his wife remained together for a further seven months. Police patrols around the area of the shop continued throughout that time. Then, on 1 January 1893, Sarah Sadler returned to Streatham police station. In a brief report made one day later, Boswell informed senior officers that her husband had taken lodgings at 108 Faraday Street, Walworth Road, Camberwell. The long marriage had reached its end. In his later report the sergeant added a footnote: 'The wife appears to desire that he should still remain under surveillance.'

Whether surveillance continued is not known; there is no further documentary evidence that police maintained a visible presence outside the shop, but is likely that they did. James Thomas Sadler was, after all, one of only two men that could have murdered Frances Coles beneath Arch 45 at Swallow Gardens. The second was the infamous 'Jack the Ripper'.

The events of late 1891 between Sadler and his wife in that shop on Danbrook Street, and the twelve months that followed, suggest that when Chief Inspector Swanson, Inspector Henry Moore, Superintendent Thomas Arnold, and Inspector Edmund Reid had put together the original case against him perhaps they were not so wide of the mark. Clearly, Sadler, in the two years that had passed since Frances Coles's horrific murder, had been unable to adapt to change. Considering the significant upturn in his general circumstances, it is difficult to understand why.

For Sadler, these past years had, to some extent, been successful, certainly, on the retailing front where he had proven his ability to run and maintain a successful business. Where he floundered was in his utter inability to restore and repair his broken family life. This lack of self-control and penchant for violence as a means of solving disputes ensured any stability and wealth he might have enjoyed remained well beyond his reach. Reinforcing, perhaps, the police's perceived view that Sadler's involvement in the cruel murder beneath that arch at Swallow Gardens was more in character than the inquest jury had believed. Sarah Sadler had laid bare the flaw within his character. He was a man with a temperament full of faults and imperfections, quick to anger, hard to please, violent when provoked. The man who, from that point on, would forever be referred to by those that never knew him as: 'The man accused of Frances Coles's Murder'.

The lasting question for the police in 1893, as that marriage broke apart, was 'could James Sadler really be the killer of Frances Coles?'

Chapter 17

Doctor Forbes Winslow

Tant here were many who disagreed. Since Ernest Thompson described hearing those retreating footsteps moving away from the dark, damp, interior of that miserable archway, many people remained convinced there was only ever one killer. This almost mystical being moved freely through Whitechapel's labyrinth of streets, killing women he had probably never met, never shared a drink with and never known by name. A street killer. A man who selected his victims from amongst women selling themselves for a few coppers late at night. Unaffected by weather, rarely seen, with an extensive knowledge of Whitechapel's street layout, its working populace, the occupations they followed and the location of the area's key industries. A man accomplished in the silent art of killing: Jack the Ripper.

Dr Forbes Winslow probably shared that same view. No crank, no oddball or attention-seeking fanatic attracted to murder for publicity, though it is fair to say he had a sense of the dramatic. He was often sought out by reporters needing to fill column inches, hoping a psychological addition to the lurid detail of murder would aid their readership; something the doctor was more than willing to provide. Much used by the courts, particularly in high-profile cases, the first of which was probably what the press headlined as *The Penge Mystery*. This was a murder that dominated newspapers in 1877 because of the appalling nature of the crime committed by a whole family, the Stauntons. Between them, Louis Staunton, his brother Patrick, along with his wife Elizabeth and her sister Alice Rhodes had supposedly starved to death Louis's wife, Harriett, in order that they could obtain her money. All had been convicted and sentenced to death at their trial at the Old Bailey. Forbes Winslow's involvement in support of a public campaign against the verdicts helped free Alice and get the death sentence on the others commuted to life imprisonment. He, like Montagu Williams, was also involved in the Percy Lefroy Mapleton case, and figured in the case against Florence Maybrick who was initially found guilty of poisoning her husband, the sentence being later commuted to life, plus the widely publicised case of Sir George Jessell, Master of the Rolls, to name but a few. Here was a Victorian psychiatrist with a psychological approach to murder and those who perpetrated it.

Born in 1844 to a wealthy middle-class family, he carried his father's name and followed in the same profession. Forbes Winslow senior, who died in 1874, had studied medicine in New York, graduated in Aberdeen and practised in London. Elected Fellow of the Royal College of Physicians, Edinburgh and Lettsomian Professor of Medicine for 1851–2, he was also an author and was known by the Royal College of Physicians of London as a doctor specialising in the treatment of insanity, diseases of the brain and of the nervous system. An illustrious background, which ensured his son received an education worthy of the family name and a career that would follow reasonably closely to that of his father. After the death of his mother in 1883, fully qualified in psychiatry by this time and practising successfully, Forbes Winslow took over the management of two asylums owned by the family: Sussex House and Brandenburg House, which stood opposite each other in Hammersmith, at a salary of £1,600 per year – the equivalent today of an annual income of around £131,000. They would prove costly acquisitions when his father's estate was eventually contested by the rest of his family, and his involvement in their running severely criticised, forcing, in turn, his bankruptcy and liabilities in excess of £14,000.

Not that this financial setback appears to have caused him too many sleepless nights. His career remained very much on track and, when the Ripper struck in the summer of 1888, he was close at hand to give advice to the investigating force, despite their reluctance to accept it. As far as Forbes Winslow was concerned, there may have been a mystery regarding the killer's identity but none as far as his mental state was concerned. He reported: 'I have a very wide experience of lunatics of all descriptions, and I am perfectly convinced, from everything I see, that the perpetrator of these crimes is a lunatic.'

This diagnosis was much quoted by the press, and he did not deviate from it over the years, though he continued to develop his view of how the killer operated and how he had remained undetected. Something, as the years went by after the well-publicised serial killing spree of 1888, he found harder to comprehend. To his mind, catching the Ripper ought to have been much easier than indicated by the newspaper reports of the day. He often argued, in his press interviews, that the Whitechapel killer proved so elusive because police were not paying attention to the clues offered up by the public.

Large numbers of letters had arrived at his town house in Wimpole Street offering names, places, occupations and ideas relating to the Ripper and by 1889 he began to develop plans of his own. Some of these he shared in an interview published by *The Sheffield and Rotherham Independent,* in which he claimed he was closing in on a suspect. He even produced a pair of snow boots which he claimed had been owned by the Ripper and carried actual blood stains to prove it: 'They were made for a very large foot, and had India rubber soles for the purpose of deadening the sound of the footsteps.'

According to the news reporter, the boots had uppers made of a strong cloth and there were no laces. He described the so-called bloodstains: 'Inside one of the boots was a faint mark which the doctor said he had ascertained by test to be blood,' also implying in his article that the doctor also supported the notion put forward by a number of amateur sleuths: that Jack had a partner, a man that worked with him. A man the newspapers called 'The Dodger'.

The story was considered apocryphal, especially as the name of the source and origin of the boots were initially omitted. But as a new development? Probably no worse than all the other theories that had found their way into newspapers over the previous year or so and maybe not completely without merit.

By the start of the 1890s, Forbes Winslow had become the go-to doctor for both the press and the public at large. He was unafraid of ridicule and more than willing to explain his views on what he perceived to be the only killer operating in the East End throughout the 1880s, and the motivations that drove him, stating: 'Well, I am convinced that he is a homicidal lunatic who is suffering from religious mania.' This was a view he had espoused since the start of the killings about a murderer that, to his mind at least, had never really gone away. Neither had he committed suicide or died of disease at the end of 1888 as was often speculated. The death of Alice McKenzie he pointed out, was probably a reawakening and murderous continuation of what had gone before and so possibly was the murder of Frances Coles, which meant James Sadler, if his theory was right, had played no part in the Swallow Gardens' murder, simply because it had been proven he was not the Ripper. Forbes Winslow never stated that publicly, perhaps preferring to stay well clear of the debate over her probable killer, content enough, perhaps, to maintain his view there had only ever been one Whitechapel murderer whilst at the same time maintaining a level of ambiguity over exactly which women were this killer's victims.

London solicitor George Kebble challenged this view of a killer still at large after the ex-Assistant Commissioner of the Metropolitan Police, Sir Robert Anderson, reportedly made the claimed that the Ripper was a Jewish man who evaded prosecution because the only witness to his guilt was of the same faith, and he had refused to testify against a fellow believer. Kebble took exception to the idea the killer was Jewish and insisted the claim was untrue. The Ripper, according to him, was an Irishman, arrested after being caught in the act of attacking a woman with a knife in February 1895. The man in question, though not named by Kebble, is today believed to have been William Grant Grainger. He appeared in court in March 1895 accused of attacking Whitechapel prostitute Alice Graham and stabbing her in the abdomen. At the time, claims were made, particularly by the press, in support of him being the Ripper and an extensive examination was mounted into the man's past. The fact he was caught red-handed, in the dead of night, in the right place, makes the claim easy to understand but not credible. There were differences in how this attack had taken place compared with how the Ripper operated. There was nothing silent in how Grainger had struck, Alice Graham had been able to shout out, her throat had not been cut and she survived the attack; something Dr Forbes Winslow was probably all too well aware of. For him, the notion that either man could have even ventured to step into the Ripper territory was too much to take without a response of some kind. After all, he was regarded by many as one of the foremost minds working in criminal psychology at the time, even if the science had never been officially fully explored or considered real amongst police circles, which he believed had earned him the right – leastways as far as the press was concerned. He seized the opportunity they provided to state publicly that both men were wrong:

> I beg to challenge the observations which have appeared during the last few days relative to the announcement that 'Jack the Ripper' was captured. If there is anyone who should know as to this I claim to be that person. The last murder committed was Alice McKenzie, on July 17, 1889.

He went on to explain, as he had tried to do many times before, he knew more about the Ripper and how he operated around Whitechapel throughout 1888 and claimed that he had stayed at one lodging house throughout most of that period. The theory was not his own but had been developed from information he received from a lodging housekeeper in late 1888 or early 1889. Forbes Winslow was not clear on the date but did accept the keeper's belief the Whitechapel killer rented a room at his house. In fact, so convinced was Forbes Winslow by this man's story and description of a well-dressed lodger, a man of 'well to do', status, as he put it, who owned eight or nine suits of clothes and changed his look daily, that he informed Scotland Yard. They listened but refused to act, reacting to information from the public perhaps being not one of their strong points. This was despite Forbes Winslow explaining the lodger also held unsavoury, contentious views about both religion and prostitution – which fit the killer profile he had previously drawn up – and would be attending the Sunday morning service at St Paul's Cathedral.

These were clear indicators to Forbes Winslow of a man suffering from severe mental decline and an obvious candidate for the police's wanted list. Half a dozen officers scattered around the cathedral steps on the upcoming Sunday would end the Ripper's reign of terror, was how he saw it. But his plea fell on deaf ears. Frustrated, and more to punish their indecision than to support his own theory, he decided to hand it over to the public. He paid a visit to the London office of the *New York Herald*, who he was confident would be supportive, and they were; they printed the story on the following day. This proved counterproductive to the murder enquiry (were there any truth behind his story) because the column inches dedicated to his story alerted the mysterious lodger and, according to the doctor, he fled. On the plus side though, that allowed the lodging housekeeper to feel free to give Forbes Winslow unfettered access to the room he had paid for. Once there, he claimed he found three pairs of women's shoes, the pair of snow boots or rubber shoes as he later described them, and a quantity of 'bows, feathers and flowers', worn generally, he believed, by the women described as the Whitechapel killer's preferred victims:

> I know his haunts, his ways of living, and his habits. He was a religious, homicidal monomaniac. Every Sunday morning he was to be seen on the steps of St Paul's Cathedral … What became of him after I had frightened him away remains my story which will never be fathomed.

Truth or lie? Forbes Winslow believed avidly it was true. Others felt differently. Either way, it does not involve Sadler. He, as far as his own story allows, played no part in the Whitechapel murders. Certainly, in later life, Forbes Winslow ignored the murder of Frances Coles in his summing up of the Ripper's murder spree. Probably for him there was nothing in the Frances Coles murder that pointed directly at the Ripper's involvement. Nor was there anything to suggest his killer profile, much publicised in the latter part of the nineteenth century, fitted her suspected murderer, James Sadler. A man who never showed any signs of being in the grip of a religious fervour; nothing, as far as is known, was ever found in his lodgings in support of that notion. But there are similarities in the way the wounds were inflicted, the time of night and way the killer eluded a heavy police presence. There is also the fact that her killer was never found, and that Forbes Winslow could have been wrong.

Perhaps the idea that he knew the identity of the most famous serial killer in history was just wishful thinking on his part. There is no reason to doubt his integrity when it comes to the Ripper and his belief he had some knowledge as to his movements. Whether or not he ever fully explained those to the detectives at Leman Street police station, as he suggested that he had, and whether they ever listened, is debatable. But some of what he went on to say over the years before his death in 1913 does stand up to scrutiny depending, of course, upon how the Jack the Ripper story is viewed.

Winslow was contentious, purposefully so. He wanted the man to be caught and was willing to expound his thoughts and theories to any that would listen. For him it was tragic that police who, we might suppose, he believed were inept, had failed to lay a glove on a man who seemed to kill at will. In turn, it probably helped formulate the idea in his mind and, as previously noted, in the minds of many others that Whitechapel's killer had somehow left the capital, maybe sailed away. Others continued to suggest he was dead, or in a mental asylum. Forbes Winslow seemed to have preferred the notion of Whitechapel's killer boarding a ship and emigrating to find a new home far away from London. The idea was not without supporters but also begs the question: had he travelled as a passenger or as a sailor working his passage?

In an interview the psychiatrist gave to the *Derry Journal*, 23 September 1895, in support of his killer with psychopathic tendencies or suffering from lunacy, as he put it, he suggested the phases of the moon affected his mood and were in some way responsible for altering his mental state. Each of what he believed to be beyond doubt the Ripper killings, matched a moon phase he felt was significant:

Martha Tabram, August 7, 1888, New Moon arising
Polly Nicholls, August 31, 1888, Moon entered its last quarter
Annie Chapman, September 8, 1888, New Moon
Elizabeth Stride, September 30, 1888, Moon entered last quarter
Catherine Eddowes, September 30, 1888, Moon entered last quarter
Mary Jane Kelly, November 9, 1888, New Moon

Fanciful maybe but not without merit. The phases of the moon's cycle when applied to the murders as published by the newspaper do perhaps raise questions. It is intriguing that Martha Tabram is shown as a definite Ripper case but not Alice McKenzie (which he had always suspected of being the last), when the moon was entering its last quarter. The omission of Frances Coles (also moon entering last quarter) from the list is perhaps more understandable. Her inclusion would have meant his theory of having forced the killer to leave London lost credibility, not something he would have wanted to do.

But, despite these musings and the perceived mysticism behind them, there is a second reason for looking closely at the phases of the moon and its possible involvement in the killings. The Thames is tidal; the moon's influence on river levels and how their rise and fall influenced sailing times is possibly significant and something perhaps more relevant to Whitechapel's killer than its effect on his mood, especially if he used the sea as an escape route, as Forbes Winslow suspected.

Clearly the doctor was, essentially, an amateur detective with a good bit of medical knowledge. He was probably also an obsessive and, as can be seen from his record of involvement in murder trials, attracted to the mechanics of murder. So much so, that throughout the latter part of 1888, at the height of the Whitechapel murders, he was even out on the streets at night playing the policeman. According to his own reported testimony, he knew the people, the police and the area extremely well by the time he stopped: 'Day after day and night after night I spent in the Whitechapel area. The detectives knew me, the lodging housekeepers knew me, the poor creatures of the streets came to know me.'

So, in many ways, his story, his idea of who the Ripper might have been; how he operated, where he lived, how he moved around and how easy it had been to strike terror into a whole community, demands a little credit. He was there, he saw and knew the place, understood how it all worked. The sights, sounds, smells, pubs, coffee houses and streetlamps were familiar. Arguably, he was nearer to the killer than the police ever were. Of course, it does not mean he was correct in everything he had to say about the place. Much of what he told reporters were assumptions with no real, hard science behind them. But there may have been a degree of logic in his reasoning. Although the first to suggest the killer was a madman or perhaps had some connection to the sea – others had made the same claim – he was just perhaps more vociferous and convincing; his background in treating mental illness more demanding of respect than others voicing the same conclusions.

In the summer of 1910, in a report in *The Courier,* Forbes Winslow reiterated his earlier theory that the killings stopped, not because the Ripper had died but because he had left the area. He showed the reporter a letter he had received claiming it provided evidence the killer had boarded a ship and left the country but was otherwise still alive and well. He even offered up detail of the letter as proof should police want to investigate the claim. They did not. As far as can be verified they made no attempt to follow up the story. For them at that late stage in enquiries, the murders being some twenty years old, there probably seemed little point in chasing up another Forbes Winslow, Jack the Ripper lead. So, the story faded away and three years later, Winslow was dead. The public lost a voice that was often thought provoking, often entertaining, sometimes misguided and always intriguing. It was a loss to what had become by that time a captivating, unfathomable mystery.

PART FOUR

THE CANONICAL FIVE

Chapter 18

Mary Ann Nichols, 31 August 1888

So, with Forbes Winslow's undying belief that only one man had committed the murders in Whitechapel and the coroner's verdict exonerating James Sadler, who killed Frances Coles? If James Sadler, living a life behind the counter in his chandler's shop at the start of summer 1891, had not killed her then had she died at the hands of the Ripper? Support for her death as the last in the Ripper's reign of horror is mixed. As we have seen with the good doctor, he seems to have been ambivalent in his view that 1891 marked the closing act, to use a theatrical phrase. For him, as he stated publicly, the Alice McKenzie murder marked the end of the Ripper's reign of terror, for others, even today, Frances Coles. Once it was decided by Mr Wynne Baxter's court that Sadler had not been her killer, the press was in no doubt the Ripper had struck again.

To understand whether or not the latter stands up to scrutiny, it is necessary to understand who the 'canonical five' were and why they have a relevance to the Coles murder. There can be no doubting the fact a serial killer was operating around Whitechapel in the 1880s. The questions most often asked are: was this man a lone killer? and if so, did he murder all the victims in that decade? Or was he only responsible for the murders centred in the summer and early winter of 1888? In other words, were the famous canonical five the only victims of the Ripper or are there similarities between those and all the others?

Of course, much has been written about the Ripper over the years – who he could have been, how he operated and the murders he committed. Particular emphasis is placed on the five women at the heart of the legend. It is not my intention here to revisit old ground, rehash well-established views, nor cover the detail behind these killings in any great depth. Others have done this and, in many cases, done it extremely well. But it is useful to simply recount and summarise, look at each of these key murders objectively to try and see how Frances Coles fits into the overall narrative of the Ripper and the way he dominated Whitechapel over 130 years ago.

When the first attributable murder took place, that of Mary Ann Nichols (Polly to those who had known her) on 31 August 1888, it caused no great alarm. 'Jack' had not been invented and there was no clear indication that there had been other similar murders in the past, nor that her death marked the start of something unprecedented. That does not mean there was an absence of murder in the area. Emma Smith had died as a result of an attack in April and Martha Tabram had been found stabbed to death in the early hours of 7 August, both that same year. These two women were known to have worked as prostitutes but neither death showed traits that would have marked them as being attributable to one killer. Emma died in hospital from injuries sustained after being attacked in the street by men thought to have belonged to one of Whitechapel's notorious street gangs. Tabram on the other hand was thought to have been murdered by a man, or men, in uniform. So, it's clearly not easy to see or believe any link existed between these two deaths and that of Mary Nichols.

In fact, when Mary Nichols was found there were no obvious, visible indications that she had actually been murdered. She lay on her back in front of the gated entrance to a Mr Brown's stable yard and coach houses on Bucks Row. It was around half past three in the morning and a gloomy, dark start to the day when she was first seen by Charles Cross on his way to work. He thought she was injured or drunk. He was joined within minutes by Robert Paul taking the same route, who agreed. The two men had a discussion as to what she was doing there, whether she was alive or dead. Cross felt her hands which were cold and thought the latter but then thought he had detected movement. So, the two men decided not to move her but to resume their journey to their respective places of employment and inform a constable en route, which they did. Though Paul, in his later statement to police added her dress had been pulled up when he first saw her, and he had pulled it down to maintain her dignity. PC Jonas Mizen, the police officer they eventually met, was not made aware of that fact nor the woman's desperate state. According to his later statement, that lack of information tempered his initial response.

Meanwhile, at around 3.45 a.m., PC John Neil had already entered Bucks Row on his nightly round. Brown's business was on his list of places to check which led him to Mary's body probably within minutes of Cross and Paul leaving her. He quickly identified that she was dead and, using his bulls eye lamp, was able to attract the attention of PC John Thain on the adjoining beat. Between the two of them they carried out another quick assessment then Thain went off to fetch Rees Llewellyn, a local doctor who they knew lived on Whitechapel Road. PC Mizen arrived as he left and Neil sent him to notify Bethnal Green police station, which was the nearest, and whilst there collect and return with an ambulance cart.

At that point, none of these policemen knew for certain Mary Nichols had been murdered despite finding blood had pooled around the body. That was only confirmed minutes later by Dr Llewellyn who, after a brief examination, deduced she had sustained a wound to her throat. When PC Mizen returned to the murder scene with the ambulance cart and Sergeant Kirby in tow, Llewellyn had the body removed and taken to the mortuary at Whitechapel Infirmary Workhouse in Eagle Place – probably the first serious error in the investigation into Mary Nichols's murder. The body ought to have been left in situ and the murder site itself more thoroughly examined. As it was, within minutes of the body's removal, an employee from Brown's yard, James Green, was out swilling away the blood and a crowd had been allowed to form around the site, destroying any evidence that could have remained. All police had to work with from that point on, were the noted observations of PC Neil, first officer on the scene. He had inspected the ground around where Mary Nichols's body had lain reasonably thoroughly whilst waiting for others to arrive. From those observations, he ascertained there were no wheel tracks or other marks visible on the road before the site itself was trampled over. A clear enough indicator she had been murdered where found and not killed elsewhere and her body carried into Bucks Row, crucial information to the later realisation her death had marked the first in a series of murders that would spread fear and panic across the whole of Whitechapel.

But that was in the future. At that early hour of the morning, when her body arrived at the mortuary there was no known urgency. Her body remained outside, lying on the ambulance cart, the mortuary still securely locked up whilst police went off to locate the mortuary attendant. The delay prompted Inspector Spratling, who waited alongside the cart, to begin a cursory examination of Mary's body and draw up an inventory of her belongings – standard police practice. According to his notes, a search of her pockets revealed a broken mirror, a piece of comb and no money. He paused momentarily when the mortuary attendant arrived to unlock the doors, then continued his examination after Mary's body had been carried inside. At that point he lifted her dress to assess her underwear, again standard procedure, and saw what everyone else had missed. Mary Nichols had been disembowelled. Dr Llewellyn was immediately called back from his home.

Clearly, as she had lain in that gated entry with apparently no clear visible loss of blood and her clothes rearranged because Robert Paul had wanted to restore her modesty, there had been no outward signs that savagery of this magnitude had been inflicted on her body, something perhaps Llewellyn ought to have seen had his examination been anything other than cursory.

As his later report detailed, she had died as a result of two stab wounds to left side of her neck; one 4 inches long from below her left ear, and a second cut an inch below that ran all the way around her neck, terminating 3 inches below her right ear. So devasting would these have been, severing all the tissue down to the vertebrae and cutting through the carotid artery on the left side, that she would have died almost instantly. According to Dr Llewellyn, that would also explain why there had never been a scream or shout. Mary Nichols never stood a chance. Examination of her clothes also revealed that they had not necessarily absorbed all the blood from the neck wound, nor from the wounds to her abdomen. The neck wound had bled into the street and beneath the body, which explained the lack of a visible blood pool when she was first found. The cuts to the abdomen had been inflicted after death and the blood had run into the stomach cavity. One extensive wound on the left side inflicted in a jagged manner but very deep, then several incisions running across the abdomen and three or four on the right made in a downward cutting motion. All, according to the doctor, made with a knife and all from left to right, possible indicators that led him to conclude her killer had been left-handed.

It was a gruesome, horrific and extremely violent death and for police at that stage also a death without precedent. Nothing in the East End or elsewhere seemed to match the kind of injuries this woman had sustained, and from a killer who left behind no clues. Initial speculation was her death, like that of Emma Smith, had been at the hands of a local gang. Police were aware of prostitutes in the area that had been victims of extortion and violence from local gangs in the past. But this theory was later dismissed, possibly on the grounds that the kind of violence they had seen before bore no resemblance to what had subsequently been inflicted on Mary Nichols.

Local police inspector, Joseph Helson, who was under an obligation to maintain a link with Scotland Yard as a matter of protocol, was reported to have held the opinion that the earlier two murders, Smith and Tabram, could have been connected but had no explanation as to how. The Yard's Inspector Abberline, who attended the eventual inquest, was believed to have shared the same view. But whether they discussed their opinion is not known. Whatever their thoughts, none of which were widely circulated it would appear, it is fair to say neither man had ever been involved in a murder investigation of this gravity before and however they went about trying to unravel the events of the 31 August, they were never likely to fully understand the significance of the case before them until perhaps much later in the Ripper enquiry. When there had been more deaths, more evidence there was more of a realisation that this murder had been the start of a worldwide exposure for the capital and the policing of it. However, at the start of their investigation, with no clear link established, all investigations were, understandably, centred solely on just who Mary Ann Nichols was.

Identification came quickly, labels in some of her clothing had come from Lambeth Workhouse and enquiries there gave them the name, Mary Nichols and her common name, Polly, which was adopted by the newspaper reporters of the day in their descriptions of the murder victim. It was also the name known to the workhouse who told police she had been an inmate back in 1887 when life had proven too difficult to stay on the street. According to Edward Walker, Mary's father, who lived in Camberwell and had discovered his daughter's death from those same reports, his daughter had been a stranger for three years. He told police she was 42 years old, had been married and had five children, one of whom lived with him and four who, he believed, were still living with her ex-husband. Their ages ranged from the eldest at 21 to the youngest between 8 or 9. The marriage had fallen apart, he explained, because during Mary's pregnancy the couple had brought in a nurse to help throughout her confinement. The nurse and Mary's husband had begun an affair; devastating for Mary, catastrophic for the children, and the cause of the marriage failure.

William Nichols, the ex-husband, was quickly located and added a little more detail after police found him living in Coburg Road, off the old Kent Road A journeyman printer by trade he worked in Fleet Street. He was brought to the mortuary and confirmed the identity already made by his ex-father-in-law. The marriage, he agreed, had broken up after some twenty-two years, both having lived apart for the last eight of those years. But he denied having caused the rift that split them up and insisted it had come about because of Mary's increasing dependency upon alcohol.

A spiral into what was probably alcoholism had begun five or six years earlier and, according to Neil R. A. Bell *Capturing Jack the Ripper*, was probably brought about after her husband stopped paying maintenance. When the marriage ended, four of the children had apparently stayed with their mother initially, not with their father. But at some point, William had refused to keep paying and had taken the case of his disputed maintenance payments to court and won, claiming she had been living off immoral earnings. For Mary Ann Nichols, with no means of earning, and dependent on alcohol, where else was she to go other than Whitechapel's streets? Earning money like thousands of others, selling her body for the price of a bed and as a result, her sordid, cruel death in that gateway.

The murder investigation into how or why, as with the cases that followed, resulted in no arrests. The puzzle was then, as it is today, what drew her to Bucks Row? What took her to that locked gateway outside Brown's stables? Just like in the Frances Coles murder that followed three years later, why did she go to the place in which she met her death?

No one was ever identified as being in company with Mary that night. At the inquest held, of course, at the Working Lads' Institute and presided over by Wynne Baxter, that lack of suspects, or witnesses to her movements prior to her murder, was in some ways highlighted by the number of witnesses who had been in or around the area after it had taken place. Walter Purkiss, who lived opposite the murder site, told the court that neither he nor his wife had heard anything. Alfred Mulshaw, night watchman who had been on duty that night in Winthorpe Street, around 50 yards away, until 6 a.m. also saw and heard nothing. PC Neil explained how he had passed the bottom of Bucks Row every thirty minutes that night and neither saw nor heard anything, whilst Charles Cross and Robert Paul told of how deserted the streets were on that walk to work at 3.30 a.m.

How did she get there unseen, die without a sound, and her killer calmly walk away? Questions as confounding today as they were then and questions that would be asked repeatedly as the Ripper enquiries picked up speed over the following weeks. Never successfully answered, obviously, escape being the most unfathomable circumstance common to each of the murders.

In the Polly Nichols case at least, there has been speculation in recent years that the man who found the body first could well have been her killer. There is perhaps some merit in that claim. Charles Cross would certainly have had the opportunity. It would appear his arrival at that gate was also unseen by nearby witnesses and several minutes ahead of Robert Paul. Their decision not to move her, not to call for help and not to explain their discovery clearly to PC Mizen, perplexing. It would seem they allowed him to believe she was anything but dead, which in turn slowed down his response. Ensuring, in turn, that PC John Neil's discovery was more fortuitous than it otherwise would have been.

But, if Cross killed her, he must also have killed all the rest, or so the argument goes. Always a possibility, the claim has been made that he did pass close by the other eventual murder sites over the following weeks. But we may suppose – so did many others.

Chapter 19

Annie Chapman, 8 September 1888

At the inquest into Mary Ann Nichols's murder, Coroner Wynne Baxter suggested a possible link between her murder and that of both Emma Smith and Martha Tabram. There were no serious grounds for making that connection. Any correlation between those two, on the surface at least, was non-existent. The coroner's observation of a possible link existing between all three killings was probably based simply on the proximity of Mary Nichols's murder to that of the other two. Perhaps three murders in four months were a more obvious cause for concern rather than the link between them, something perhaps Whitechapel's police were more accepting of rather than any connection.

Certainly, the discovery of Mary Ann Nichols's body did not automatically set alarm bells ringing. The wounds inflicted on her in no way matched those of the two earlier victims. Therefore, to police eyes at least it was safe to assume the same killer, despite the coroner's suspicions, had not struck three times. The notion of a serial killer operating around the district managed by Whitechapel's police at that time was never a consideration. The area was already dangerous by repute, riven by poverty, prostitution, theft and violence, frequently fuelled by a daily influx of cash-rich sailors brought into the docks on the day's high tide. Violent death, therefore, was not wholly unexpected in the area and perhaps seen by some as the price to be paid for living on the edge. This view changed radically after the discovery of Annie Chapman's body in the yard at the back of 29 Hanbury Street on the morning of 8 September.

The house itself was rented out to Amelia Richardson. She in turn sub-let the rooms and had around sixteen or seventeen tenants sharing her space. Capable, astute and with a religious bent she, along with her son, John, ran a packing-case business that had originally been set up by her husband. She had a good relationship with her lodgers, many of whom had lived with her for years. The front door to the house opened into a corridor that ran the length of the ground floor, ending at a second door allowing access into a back yard. The yard itself lay some 3 or 4 feet below the level of the passageway and was reached via two stone steps. The positioning of those steps created a recess between themselves and the rear doorway. The body of Annie Chapman, or dark Annie as she was known, was found in that recess.

John Davis, who shared a room with his wife and family on the third floor, had been awakened by the chiming of the clock above Spitalfields' church at about 5.45 a.m. Employed at Leadenhall market and an early riser, he had gone downstairs to make tea. Once in the passage on the ground floor he found the front door wide open, which was not unusual, and the rear door closed. Access to the house had purposely never been secure as most of the lodgers were employed and left the house at various times throughout the early hours of the morning. Locking the doors, therefore, was deemed impractical, which obviously suited the residents and was never objected to by the Richardson family.

Whether because he wanted to use the outside toilet or just wanted to take in the morning air, Davis made his way through the rear door and out into the yard. The sight that met him probably stayed with him for the rest of his life. Annie Chapman's body had been arranged in such a way it would cause maximum distress to whoever found her. Her head lay towards the house, her legs were drawn up with her feet on the ground. Her clothes had been lifted to expose her abdomen, which had been slit open, her throat cut, and a section of her intestines had been removed and placed over her right shoulder; a large part of her stomach had been cut away and placed over her left shoulder.

Unlike Mary Ann Nichols this murder was designed to horrify and shock in a way that, even looking at it today, is truly barbaric.

John Davis's reaction was understandable. He ran back into the house, along the passage, out through the front door and into the street. Once there he found Henry Holland, a man on his way to work, and two men standing outside the Black Swan pub. Understandably animated and probably in shock at what he had seen, he tried to explain what he had found and persuaded them to follow him back into the house and out into the back yard. The commotion brought landlady, Mrs Richardson, from her bed and within minutes a crowd of onlookers had gathered at the front of the house. Their shouts alerted Inspector Joseph Chandler who had been attending to another matter nearby. In his later notes he recorded the time as being around twenty minutes past six. After a cursory look in the back yard, he had someone go and find divisional surgeon Dr George Phillips and sent word back to Commercial Road police station.

By 6.30 a.m. Dr Phillips was on scene; other constables arrived to control the growing crowd and help protect the murder site and by 7 a.m. the investigation was under way. For obvious reasons it was a particularly difficult crime scene to evaluate. There had been no murder exhibiting this level of barbarity ever seen in Whitechapel. So, for police and the case doctor alike it proved incredibly difficult to properly assess what they were dealing with. In his initial examination, given the nature of the injuries he was confronted with, and which could only have been cursory at best, he deduced there had been no struggle. Annie Chapman had been alive, in his opinion, when she had entered that back yard but had somehow been rendered insensible before her throat was cut. At such an early stage of the enquiry, police had no reason to doubt his conclusions and it remained a version of events that was never contested. Throughout the whole investigation, no witness ever came forward with evidence of hearing shouts or raised voices at any point that morning. As with the Frances Coles murder and others still to come, no one saw or heard anything. The most contentious issue, as it was in Swallow

Gardens three years later, was time of death. Trying to assess exactly when the killing had taken place proved difficult from the start. The doctor's initial thoughts on time were that she had died some two hours before he had arrived. But later enquiries challenged the accuracy of that assessment after it was shown there had been too much movement in and around the house and back yard between four and six o'clock that morning for it to be correct.

The landlady's son, John Richardson, told police he had been sitting outside the rear door at around 4.45 a.m. cutting leather away from one of his shoes, and the body had not been there then. Near neighbours claimed to have seen Annie with a man in Hanbury Street at around 5.30 a.m. Another, Albert Cadosch, thought he had heard a woman talking to someone at about 5.15 a.m. outside the house. All of which clouded the issue of time of death and meant, despite what Dr Phillips believed, there was never going to be an accurate time recorded for the murder. Therefore, trying to assess and understand her movements throughout the previous night in question became more crucial than it otherwise would have been.

Obviously, investigations were underway within minutes of her body being carried away on the ambulance cart to the mortuary in Old Montague Street. Initial thoughts by those involved were probably that her movements ought to be reasonably easy to follow. Identity was never a problem, she was known locally, had been living at a lodging house at 35 Dorset Street and drank in the nearby public houses. Timothy Donovan, deputy of the lodging house, claimed to have known her well; she had lived there for some time paying 8d a night for a bed. Drink, according to him, was at times her problem. She liked a rum and occasionally a man, 'a pensioner', stayed with her. On the night of her death, Donovan told police, she had turned up at the lodging house about 1.40 a.m. alone, worse the wear for drink and looking for a room but with no money to secure it. The house agreed she could have a bed but only if she paid and she had told the night watchman, 'I haven't enough now but keep my bed for me. I shan't be long.'

Where she went, who she met and how she ended up in the back yard of 29 Hanbury Street was never known. Intense investigations uncovered little more. What police did discover was that Annie Chapman's life had not always been lived with the same sense of desperation. She had, some years earlier, lived at Windsor married to a coachman, Frederick Chapman, who worked for a gentleman living near the royal borough. She had a daughter whose education at an unnamed, 'highly respectable', ladies' school had been properly funded. The girl's childhood had seen no serious financial worries and at the time of her mother's death she was thought to be living in France. She also had a son, born with a handicap and living as an inmate of a home, again not named in police reports. Neither had seen their mother for some years and appeared to have had no interest in doing so whilst she lived in Whitechapel. If the marriage had continued, perhaps life would have been kinder and the East End remained a foreign place. As it was, she and the coachman, for reasons never fully disclosed, found life together fraught, contentious and miserable. They eventually parted, he stayed where he was, she drifted towards life on the streets and an 8d bed in a lodging house on Dorset Street. She supported herself initially by what she could earn doing crochet work or selling flowers to supplement the 10 shillings a week her husband sent her.

For a while she lived with a man, Jack Sivvey and used his surname. The two of them lived reasonably well inside Whitechapel's harsh environment. Then her husband died at the end of 1886 and the weekly allowance stopped. She and Jack are thought to have parted at around the same time. Annie then began a relationship with a man named Edward Stanley, thought to be the man Timothy Donovan had alluded to and known to him as the pensioner. As far as is known the relationship was not serious, the two only spending every weekend together. Whether she was actively involved in prostitution throughout this time is not known. There are suggestions she was, maybe on a casual basis, but the evidence is not substantive. Neither is there significant evidence in support of her being a heavy drinker other than at weekends, despite her taste for rum.

At the time of her murder, she was 47 years old, 5ft tall, overweight, and struggling to pay for a bed every night of the week. Annie Chapman had been living a hard life. As Dr Phillips began his autopsy, he would have known before he started that she had also died a hard death. According to his later testimony at Wynne Baxter's coroner's court hearing, the mutilations were so severe they ought not to be discussed in an open courtroom: 'To make public the further results of the examination would thwart the ends of justice.'

But the coroner, quite rightly, was having none of it. For him justice would never be served if it had to hide from unpalatable truths being spoken in open court. Dr Phillips had no choice but to comply. But as he explained in brutal detail the injuries Annie Chapman had suffered, his initial reticence was easier to understand.

According to the doctor, the killer had used a knife some 5–6 inches in length to cut her throat. A long incision made from left to right. A shorter cut, parallel but beneath the first had then been made, possibly in an attempt to severe her head. Bruising to her face and scratches to her neck suggested her killer had lifted her head in order to facilitate both cuts. Mercifully, according to post–mortem evidence, only after strangulation rendered her unconscious and she had been pushed to the ground. The long incision that opened her abdomen, and which enabled the killer to lift out parts of her intestines and her stomach, had been made after death. The uterus and part of her bladder had also been removed, neither of which were found at the murder scene, which suggested her killer had carried them away.

It was a brutal murder, hard to read and difficult to comprehend. Even more so when the doctor went on to explain much of this butchery could not have been achieved without a level of anatomical knowledge, and the time to carry it out. Around fifteen minutes or more was his estimate which, as he told the court, was much faster than a good, competent surgeon, whom 'it would probably have taken the best part of one hour.'

So, how did her killer find the time at whatever hour of the morning he committed the murder, to carry out so complex an operation? A surgical mutilation was difficult to carry out in broad daylight let alone in the dark and within the confined space of the yard behind 29 Hanbury Street.

Sunrise on 8 September 1888 was 5.25 a.m. and the morning was dry and bright. John Davis had found Annie's body at a little after 5.45 a.m. Dr Phillips had arrived at 6.30 a.m. and assessed death as being two hours earlier, which put it at around 4.30 a.m. that same morning. But it was thought at the time, and still so today, his calculation was rudimentary, inaccurate and not based on sound forensic analysis. Annie Chapman had bled out hours before his arrival on the scene, which meant death could well have been much earlier than he believed. It also meant the murder, and everything done to the victim in its aftermath had taken place in moonlight.

The times offered up by witnesses to the events of that night (as with Frances Coles), just like the doctor's crime scene assessment, simply confuse. There is no best-case scenario. Witness accounts, based on the chiming of a clock on top of a church, disagree with that sequence of events. In turn, they dispute the doctor's findings, and lodging house deputy Timothy Donovan's assertion she left his house at 1.40 a.m. after securing a bed for the night, add a different and more perplexing dimension to the whole night's events.

If she died after dawn, where had she been for four hours? With her killer? Jack the Ripper, as we know him today, simply never did that – did he?

Chapter 20

Elizabeth Stride, 30 September 1888

Essentially, the man we recognise today as the Whitechapel murderer always worked in the dark. To do otherwise was illogical. It would have vastly increased his risk of being seen, recognised or stopped by police. Or was that never a concern? In other words, was he always in plain sight? It seems impossible that any murderer, then or now, was able to inflict the kind of wounds sustained by Annie Chapman and simply walk away. Yet that is exactly what appears to have happened. Somehow the Whitechapel killer, despite supposedly operating at an hour of the morning deemed by many as the start of the working day, had simply blended in unnoticed. Of course, he could have been resident in the house where she was found, and presumably police made the necessary checks, or he could simply have gone to work somewhere close by. More likely, if he killed nearer 2 a.m. than the supposed 4 or 5 a.m., he simply returned to his bed in one of Whitechapel's many lodging houses and slept until dawn. That presupposes, of course, he was *not* covered in blood. Perhaps the key to gaining insight into these murders is not so much the killing itself but the method adopted. Whoever murdered Annie Chapman, according to the crime scene descriptions, must have suffered significant bloodstaining. Leastways that is how it looks on the surface. But this killer is both professional and knowledgeable. If the same man had also killed Polly Nichols, then these two murders were premeditated. Around ninety years later, Peter Sutcliffe, the 'Yorkshire Ripper' operated in a similar way. He knew he was going to kill, had planned it, maybe even selected his victim, carried the necessary tools for the job and knew where he intended to carry out that kill. When he struck, he knew exactly what he was doing and how to minimise any incriminating evidence being left behind, or seen on his person. Even so, he ran the risk of being caught. The risk in 1888 was even higher. Whitechapel's streets were almost never empty; people worked odd hours compared to today and police were not driving around in cars and reacting to crime. They were on foot, generally only yards away from where any crime was being committed. A police constable always worked a fixed beat in close proximity to other constables patrolling nearby streets. Escape, unseen, was therefore extremely unlikely – unless the killer fully understood the working patterns and procedures of the constables. Given the way Annie Chapman had been murdered, it is likely that the Ripper had such knowledge, along with some understanding of anatomy and how the human body functions.

Surely, there was simply too much blood at her murder scene for him not to have been contaminated by it. So, why no bloody footprints? Why no blood splashes covering the nearby fence or wall? Why no bloody handprints? The only way back on to Hanbury Road was through the house. He had to open and close the rear door. If he cut out organs and carried them away, how did he manage that? What did he carry them in? How, in fact, did he have the time? Dr Phillips' court testimony of fifteen minutes to one hour, depending on the level of expertise, means Annie Chapman's killer was in no rush.

The killer, it is safe to assume, was both knowledgeable and careful. Perhaps, as the doctor suggested, he strangled, waited, cut her throat, waited, then carried out the mutilation, being careful throughout to stay clear of any contamination that would draw attention when he left the scene. Obviously, this is speculation but is worthy of some consideration. He did escape and has not been identified in more than 100 years. Do any of these observations relate to Frances Coles? Yes. No mutilation of her body of course, but he struck here as there, unseen, unheard and in the dark. But the killing that stands up to greater comparison is the one that followed Annie Chapman a few days later.

The body of Elizabeth Stride was discovered at around 1 a.m. on the morning of 30 September by Louis Diemshutz, a dealer in cheap jewellery and a regular trader on a Saturday at the Westow Hill market. The 8 miles or so back to Berner Street had been slow. Traffic from south London, no matter what time of night, was never easy to navigate. As he turned his horse and trap into the yard behind the Working Men's Educational Club, which for him was home, the horse shied away from its usual stopping point and pulled towards the left. Diemshutz stopped the trap and jumped down to investigate the cause. What he saw, he later described as being like a mound of mud. He prodded at it with his whip but only realised it was a woman's body after striking a match.

So began the next stage in the Ripper investigation.

The body lay in the shadow of the club some yards from the gated entrance marking an opening into what was known locally as Dutfield's Yard. It sat just off Berner Street. A narrow street described by the *Glasgow Evening Telegraph* as being a place occupied by 'small dwellings, in which reside a number of artisans. One of the houses is used as the International Socialist Club, and next to the club is a yard entered by two large wooden gates which always remain open.'

The yard itself gave entry into the club via a side door and was overlooked by a row of small houses. At that time of the morning, it had just concluded a meeting, chaired by Morris Eagle, about socialism and, according to the press, those attending had broken into song as the horse and trap arrived outside. The sounds of this carried across the yard, effectively drowning out any shouts of alarm, had there been any.

First police on the scene were PCs Henry Lamb and William Aycliffe. The two had been patrolling the south side of Commercial Road, near to Berner Street. In Lamb's later assessment of the murder scene, he described having to use his bulls eye lamp to illuminate the yard before he could clearly make out the body lying on its left side, her head nearest to the wall of the club. There was blood on the ground and her throat had been cut. Despite the poor light, as far as he was concerned, it was sufficient to confirm death and murder. Protocol and procedure took over from that point. Aycliffe was immediately sent off to fetch a doctor and Morris Eagle, the man alerted by Louis Diemshutz, and who had brought the policemen to the scene, was sent off to Leman Street police station to inform the duty inspector. Whilst all that was taking place, further help arrived in the form of PC William Smith, alerted by all the commotion, Berner Street being part of his nightly patrol. He was quickly sent off to fetch an ambulance cart. Henry Lamb then had the yard gates closed and waited for help to arrive.

It was not a long wait. Edward Johnson, assistant to police doctor, Frederick Blackwell, arrived within minutes. He was the first responder to PC Aycliffe's door knock at the Commercial Road surgery. Blackwell, who was otherwise engaged, had agreed to follow on. Johnson noted in his cursory examination of the scene that blood was not flowing, and the body was still warm. There were no other noted observations other than confirmation of death. Dr Blackwell arrived minutes later (recorded as being 1.16 a.m.) and took over the examination. According to a later brief interview he gave to the press, he described the injuries he saw as being to the throat, with no mutilation:

> Her head had been almost severed from her body. The body was perfectly warm, and life could not have been extinct for more than twenty minutes ... the deceased had on a black velvet jacket and a black dress. In her hand she held a box of cachous, whilst pinned in her dress was a flower.

He went on to explain how he thought the attack had taken place, certain her head had been dragged back by the killer pulling on a silk handkerchief worn around her neck. This action, he claimed, would have given him access to her throat. Blood found on her hands, he suggested, was indicative of her having struggled as he cut through her neck, severing her windpipe. The cut itself made in such a way, he told the reporter, that he doubted the wound would have resulted in any bloodstaining to the attacker.

H Division surgeon Dr Phillips later added to this version of events when he suggested it was likely Elizabeth Stride was attacked whilst on the ground with the killer positioned on her right side. The cut to her throat, he told Wynne Baxter at the later inquest, was 6 inches long and the only wound she had sustained; bruises found on her shoulders were supportive of Blackwell's notion of there having been some sort of initial struggle, the implication being that possibly her killer had been a potential client if she was working as a prostitute. Although the doctor's report on the items found on her person did not indicate prostitution, there was no money. All that had been found he listed: a padlock key; a comb; a broken piece of comb; a piece of pencil; a metal spoon; and a few old buttons.

The case for her earning a living as a working prostitute, as far as anyone knows, is unproven even if likely. The circumstances of her death certainly suggest it was a possibility. But her personal circumstances proved difficult to unravel when police began investigations into how she had lived. According to Sven Olsson, pastor of the Swedish church in Prince's Square, Elizabeth was born in a small village, near Gothenburg, Sweden in November 1843. He had known her for seventeen years and according to his account of her past life she was christened Elizabeth Gustafsdotter and had married an Englishman, John Thomas Stride, in 1869. The marriage had fallen apart over the years and she had been living with a man named Michael Kidney since 1885. The relationship, he believed, was more casual than serious, with Elizabeth disappearing for days, sometimes months, and then returning. The story was eventually confirmed by a woman named Elizabeth Tanner who owned a lodging house in Flower and Dean Street and had known Elizabeth Stride since around 1883. It tended to be Tanner's house she ran to whenever she felt the need to escape from whatever difficulties life threw up.

Both Sven Olsson and Elizabeth Tanner thought John Stride had been a sailor and they believed he had died in what was known locally as the Princess Alice disaster – a collision between the paddle steamer *Princess Alice* and the collier *Bywell Castle* on the River Thames on 3 September 1878. It was a huge disaster with a reported loss of life of between 600 and 700. The true loss was never confirmed because there were no accurate passenger lists and therefore it was impossible for authorities to be more precise. Michael Kidney, who claimed, after being located by police, to still be living with Elizabeth, confirmed the disaster story but added that not only had her husband, John, drowned but also her only two children, and she herself suffered severe damage to the upper palate of her mouth during her own rescue. All plausible and upsetting, were it true. But it was all a lie. The disaster is real enough, but her family's involvement in it is not. Elizabeth Stride never had children and police enquiries discovered John Stride had never sailed on the ship and was alive and well.

It appears Elizabeth or Long Liz as she was known locally, was not averse to being economical with the truth when it suited her. Maybe a history of hardship and loss bought her street credibility, or perhaps there was another, darker reason to have lied about her involvement in a great shipping disaster. Whatever her motive, she seems to have told the story often enough to perhaps have believed it herself. Certainly, it was never challenged and must have been the subject of occasional gossip in the pubs around where Elizabeth went drinking.

So, on the night she died where had she been? According to Michael Kidney, he had not seen her for three days. She left him on the Tuesday, 25 September, taking some of her belongings but did not explain why or where she was going. She had done it before and, he told police, he expected her to return. On the Saturday, an hour or so before her murder, labourer William Marshall, who lived on Berner Street, saw her at around 11.45 p.m., talking to a middle-aged man he described as around 5ft 6in tall, rather stout, wearing a short black coat, dark trousers and a round cap with a small peak.

Similar in appearance, he thought, to that worn by sailors. An hour later, James Brown, who lived in Fairclough Street, saw her talking to a man wearing a long, dark coat 'which reached nearly to his heels'.

Neither man was seen by local beat bobby, PC William Smith, the man who had arrived at the murder scene minutes after her body had been discovered. He made a statement to the effect he had seen her talking with a completely different man about 12.30 p.m., near to the yard in which she had been found. This man, again described as standing about 5ft 7in tall but wearing a deer-stalker hat and dark clothes, was carrying a newspaper parcel in his hand. He seemed about 28 years old and was dressed in a respectable manner.

Most probably this last observation is the more accurate, certainly it ought to be. PC Smith was a trained observer, familiar with the territory, the streets, the people he saw and the people he met. Qualities the Ripper investigation constantly lacked, which suggests this sighting was credible, and may well have been of Elizabeth Stride meeting her killer. But like all things related to the Ripper, nothing is ever that easy. A man named Israel Schwartz made a statement to police several hours after the murder in which he claimed to have seen an incident in that same gateway on Berner Street. According to what is known about that statement, he had been walking behind a man he followed into Berner Street and had seen him meet, then assault, a woman by the open gates. On the opposite side of the road was a second man, lighting a pipe. To this second man the woman called out the name Lipski. Schwartz, fearing for his own safety had not lingered and hurried on past.

Israel Lipski had been executed for murder in August 1887. The woman calling out the name may have been using it in a derogatory way. Lipski, a Polish Jew, had murdered a young woman near to Berner Street. So, it is extremely likely she was using the term as a racist slur aimed at the pipe smoker. Whether Israel Schwartz saw it the same way is not known but the more important question at the time was did he see Elizabeth Stride? It would seem likely. But the police appeared to treat his statement with some caution. Although there appears to have been no widespread publicity surrounding it, reference to it is made in a number of books whose narrative covers the Stride case. The question has to be: if Schwartz witnessed the prelude to Elizabeth Stride's murder, who did the policeman see?

There is also the question, as in the Frances Coles case, was this a Ripper murder? Dr Phillips did not think so. He found no similarities between this murder and the Annie Chapman murder of a few weeks earlier, indirectly suggesting there were two killers on the loose in London. More work would have been required to provide a conclusive link. Something that never happened because on the same night as Elizabeth Stride met her death so did Catherine Eddowes an hour or so later. This second murder was far less ambiguous its method.

Chapter 21

Catherine Eddowes, 30 September 1888

At 1.44 a.m. that same morning, three-quarters of a mile away from where Elizabeth Stride had been found on Berner Street, PC Edward Watkins walked into Mitre Square. A location described as being 'bounded on three sides by warehouses', and its cobbled street poorly lit but a key part of his beat. Those warehouses, with only one exception, had no night watchmen, their owners dependent on the constable carrying out the necessary security checks throughout the night. There was nothing complex about it: check the locks, look for lights listen for sounds. He had been doing it for seventeen years and the place was familiar, his duties routine. He followed procedure, made the checks and moved on. He walked through Mitre Square roughly every fifteen minutes.

What made this walk-through different was the body in the corner. It lay close to his entry point off Mitre Street, close to a pair of locked factory gates behind a shop that made picture frames, and opposite grocery wholesalers Messrs Kearley and Tonge's warehouse, the one business still paying for a night watchman. Holding up his bull's eye lamp he identified the dark shape of a woman, and by the quantity of blood around her correctly confirmed she was dead. According to his later statement, she was lying on her back and her dress had been pulled up to her waist. As he neared, he saw her throat was cut, her abdomen ripped open, and her face mutilated. He did not need to see anything else. From that point on he followed procedure, instructed that night watchman, a man named Morris, to go and find help whilst he stayed by the dead woman and secured the scene.

Dr George Sequeira was on the scene minutes later followed by divisional surgeon, Dr Gordon Brown. No familiar names here. This was not Metropolitan Police territory; it was City of London so did not fall to Whitechapel's H division. That may have changed how the initial investigation began but not how the case eventually unravelled. This was the Ripper in place, time, method and level of brutality. So, how things were done was key to what would happen next. Whether that pressure was reflected in how the two doctors carried out their on-site examination can only be imagined, but it is likely to have made an impact. The barbarity of the attack and the injuries inflicted were sufficiently savage in nature to have focused their minds and maybe even their medical conclusions. The suspect in this murder was never doubted given the picture slowly building from evidence already collected from the earlier murder sites, the Elizabeth Stride killing, which was only streets away included, even though detail as to the murder itself probably still sketchy at 2 a.m. From the moment Gordon Brown joined his fellow doctor on that cobbled street he would have known this was going to be a high-profile murder case.

According to his later report, probably the best description of what was found in Mitre Square, this killing also surpassed everything else the Ripper had done before. The report itself, made at such an early hour on a dark, cold late September morning after only a cursory examination of the scene is, nevertheless, meticulous in its detail. The body, he stated, lay with both arms by the sides. The throat had been cut once; cuts had been made to her eyes, nose and face. The lower part of her body had been exposed and there were no underclothes. She had been eviscerated and part of her intestines placed over her right shoulder; a 2ft piece placed between her left hand and her body. The lobe of her right ear was cut off and blood had clotted on the pavement on the left side of her body, above the shoulder and beneath her neck and head. He estimated time of death as being about half an hour or so before he arrived. He also observed there was no blood spurt staining found on nearby brickwork or pavement, indicative to him that she had been on the ground when killed.

All of which made the horrific murder in Mitre Square far worse than what had gone before but with clear similarities to the killings of Annie Chapman and Mary Ann Nicholls – though in the latter case the abdominal mutilations were less severe, maybe simply because the killer had less time. Nevertheless, they showed intent and demonstrated a level of psychopathic behaviour by a killer clearly intent on shock. A killer the like of which had never been seen in this country let alone London. Over the years, we seem to have sanitised these women's deaths and fictionalised them to better fit the Ripper's TV profile. But this man was savage, heartless and inhuman. The ferocity with which he attacked, never mind the mystery of how he escaped unseen, is staggering. Little wonder the police investigation had been floundering since the first killing.

But in Mitre Square there remained a clue, of sorts. A part of the dead woman's apron was missing, not noted at the scene. Understandably, it was still dark by the time the two doctors had completed that initial examination and the scene had been badly disturbed. For local inspector Edward Collard, who arrived in the square just after Dr Sequeira, organising a search of the surrounding area had been his first priority. He also had to ensure the three entrances allowing access to the square were closed off and, finally, liaise with the City Police detectives who arrived before him. So, that first, frantic hour after discovery was spent helping co-ordinate the hunt for the killer. Examining the clothes she was wearing, at that juncture, was not a priority. The damaged apron was not spotted until the body had been taken away to the Golden Lane Mortuary and matched with a piece of fabric found later.

PC Alfred Long, the man responsible for that find, did not initially realise its importance when he discovered it in Goulston Street. A piece of dirty cloth laid at the entrance to a group of new houses would probably not normally have attracted his attention. But, as he cast a light over the place where it lay and saw the chalk writing on the wall above it, the find took on a greater significance.

The scrawled message 'The Jews are the men that will not be blamed for nothing' probably meant little to PC Long when he first saw it at around 2.55 a.m. but having already been made aware of the killing in Mitre Square the obvious connotation could not be ignored. He picked up the cloth, found it to be bloodstained and noted down the wording on the wall. It was contentious then and still is today because police later had the writing wiped away, citing concern for the local Jewish population as the reason for its obliteration. Its possible connection to the piece of blood-covered fabric the constable had found was not realised until it found its way to the City Police mortuary, where it was found to match and fit the missing section of apron removed prior to the post-mortem.

Whether left by error or design, that piece of cloth was the clue – potentially crucial – because it indicated the route taken by the killer after he left Mitre Square and at the same time suggested he might have rooms in the Whitechapel area. Maybe even in Goulston Street or somewhere close by. Police wasted no time in organising a search of the buildings within a reasonable radius of its discovery. Of course, it yielded nothing, nor did early morning calls at the various lodging houses. As for the writing, it was deemed to be either a cryptic clue or completely irrelevant and remains as debatable today as it was in 1888. Hindsight suggests it should have been photographed, which is what the City Police wanted to do and not simply removed as the Metropolitan Police decided to do. Maybe it would have led to something relevant if the writing style had been compared with that of the various letters being received by both police and press. Either way, the opportunity passed, as did criticism of the decision, and the emphasis switched back to the murder victim and her identity.

By mid-morning, police had a name: Catherine Eddowes – a woman they had locked up at Bishopsgate police station after being found drunk and incapable in Aldgate High Street hours before her death. She had given her name as Mary Ann Kelly when they released her at around one o'clock that same morning. The discovery of her earlier arrest obviously helped with the identity, but it was the arrival of John Kelly at Bishopsgate police station that finally confirmed her name.

Kelly told police he had known Catherine for about seven years, and the two of them had lived as husband and wife for much of that time. Forever short of money, she earned what she could as a hawker, selling goods on the street or cleaning for local Jewish families. At the start of the week leading up to her murder the two of them had been in Kent, hop picking, but according to Kelly, they earned nothing from it and had to walk back to London. Catherine had been forced to sleep at the casual ward at Shoe Lane on the Thursday night and in the Mile End Workhouse on the Friday. So bad were their finances that by Saturday morning they had decided to pawn his working boots, raising half a crown, which they spent on food and drink. So, by Saturday afternoon they were back where they had started, poor and destitute. To try and raise more money Catherine, he told police, had decided to go and find her daughter, Anne, who lived in Bermondsey and had helped her mother before. The two of them split up at that point and he had expected her to be back at the lodging house they usually used that night. She never returned.

Frederick Wilkinson, deputy of that lodging house which stood in Flower and Dean Street, confirmed the two of them had been regular lodgers over the years, paying 8d for a bed most nights. He felt he knew the two of them reasonably well and there had been occasions in the past where they had joined the other 100 or so other lodgers in his house and, due to lack of funds, paid the 8d later. Catherine as far as he was aware, had always worked hard, liked a drink sometimes, though was rarely drunk, and did not have a history of prostitution.

The obvious question, and one police must have asked, was if she had been so short of money on the night she died, who had bought her drinks in the early evening and why? The implication was there was possibly more to it than just the alcohol. Or was it simply that Catherine had more money in her pocket than John Kelly thought?

Whatever the answer, police never discovered it. At the inquest which opened on 4 October before coroner Dr Samuel Langham, no witness had been found who could either shed light on where she had been drinking or whom she had been drinking with. Obviously, Whitechapel's drinkers could be a tight-lipped group at times. What was forthcoming was more confirmatory evidence about Catherine's immediate past, which came from her sister, Eliza Gold. She had at one time lived in Thrawl Street and was able to confirm Catherine's age as 43 and John Kelly's story of her earning a living working for a number of Jewish families in Brick Lane and selling goods on the street. What she contested was the widely held belief Catherine drank heavily. According to her that was untrue. Catherine, she told the court, had lived a sober life. But that was in direct contradiction to evidence police had already collated. Maybe it was too much for Eliza to admit, or perhaps she had not been around much in the late 1870s when, as the investigation had already uncovered, Catherine's alcohol dependence had impacted on her relationship with the father of her children, Thomas Conway. Theirs had been a stormy relationship by all accounts and Catherine's drinking habits responsible for their inevitable split at some time around 1880.

All good, solid background information, but none of it threw any light on the circumstances of her death. Catherine Eddowes had obviously been living a life of hardship and poverty, similar in almost every respect to those of the earlier victims. Whitechapel's killer, who even though on this occasion had crossed into City Police territory, appeared as careful as ever when it came to selecting his quarry. Catherine's death, as with the rest of his victims, raised more questions than it answered, the key one always being the same: How did he escape the scene?

The night watchman, Morris, added to the confusion when he explained to the coroner the night's events as he saw them and how, throughout every night shift, he was always alert to anyone entering Mitre Square. He could time the constable's nightly beat with some precision and hear his boots hit the cobbles every time he entered and left the square. Yet, when Catherine Eddowes died, he saw and heard absolutely nothing.

Listening to Morris's testimony with the same question in mind was City of London's acting commissioner, Major Henry Smith. He was standing in for Sir James Fraser who was on leave and this Ripper murder had fallen under his jurisdiction. It was an unenviable position, given that all the knowledge gained so far about how this killer operated was in the possession of H Division's officers and held in Whitechapel's Leman Street police station. Perhaps it was the key reason he attended the inquest in the first place, not that it in any way diminished or devalued the police's investigation into the murder. What was needed, which he would have recognised well enough, was closer communication with their Metropolitan colleagues.

Certainly, the doctor's testimony to the coroner's court was far more in-depth than that ever offered up by Dr Phillips. Gordon Brown's evidence was not only concise but extremely detailed. He reprised his earlier findings given to the police after his examination of the body in the early hours of the morning – all of which were reasonably insightful. But then he explained with brutal accuracy the specific nature of the wounds inflicted upon Catherine Eddowes in the shadowy darkness of Mitre Square.

The most startling features were that Catherine Eddowes's killer had removed the left kidney and a portion of her womb; in his opinion she had been on the ground when her throat was cut, and the killer had knelt down on her right side to carry out the mutilations. His statement had a chillingly familiar ring about it. So did the fact he thought the killer to be a man possessing a reasonable amount of anatomical knowledge.

Dr Brown also explained to the court what had been found on Catherine Eddowes person prior to the start of the post-mortem: a cigarette case, two clay pipes, an empty matchbox, two small tin boxes (one contained tea the other sugar), and a lengthy list of small inconsequential bits and pieces. Nothing of great significance except for the tea and sugar of course, which supported John Kelly's assertion the two of them had shopped for groceries earlier in the day. What was not found is perhaps of greater interest. Catherine Eddowes had no money on her person. Another factor which seemed in common with previous murders.

Another shared similarity was no one saw or heard anything suspicious during the crucial time period around Catherine Eddowes's death. Police carried out a thorough door-to-door enquiry in the hours immediately following the discovery. It yielded absolutely nothing. Sound sleepers all, which adds credence to the fact that the Ripper had evolved into an efficient, deadly, silent killer. A man who seemed to choose his targets and his killing ground with a degree of skill. Almost as if the meeting between victim and killer had been by appointment, the destination pre-arranged, with the killer able to maintain anonymity. A man they had never met, perhaps never seen, lured by the promise of money – lack of it being the one thing all the victims had in common.

Whether the police ever thought the same way is difficult to ascertain. Probably for them these were street killings amongst Whitechapel's most vulnerable because the trade they plied in the early hours of the morning made them so. The police's frustration after the Mitre Square murder must have been considerable. They had increased the number of officers on the beat, placed plain clothes detectives at what they believed were salient points across the district and improved the techniques deployed at murder sites, and still their inability to catch him was embarrassingly obvious. Information appears to have flowed freely around most of the East End and there had been arrests. None were of any significance, though there had been a moment when it must have felt as though a breakthrough had been achieved.

Around 5 October, a man named William Bull walked into Bishopsgate police station at twenty minutes to eleven that night and confessed to the murder of Catherine Eddowes.

> I live at Dalston. I am a medical student at the London Hospital. I wish to give myself up for the murder in Aldgate.

On Saturday night or Sunday morning about two o'clock
I think I met a woman in Aldgate. I went with her up a
narrow street not far from the main road for an immoral
purpose. I promised to give her half a crown, which I did.
While walking along together there was a second man who
came up and took the half-crown from her.

The statement sounded plausible to Inspector Izzard who carried
out the interview in the presence of Major Smith. Certainly, it was
enough to have him brought him up in court and remanded into
custody. But the confession quickly fell apart after he told police
he could not give them the clothes he had worn on the night of the
murder or the murder weapon: 'If you wish to know, they are in the
sea, and the knife I threw away.'

Follow-up enquiries also revealed he had nothing to do with the
London hospital, which for police was enough to satisfy them he was
either a fantasist or mentally ill; an assumption confirmed in part
after he later admitted the confession had been made whilst he had
been drunk, and was untrue.

From that point on, the investigation seemed to fade away as
nothing new came to light. The East End became a tourist attraction
according to the *Illustrated Weekly Telegraph*. A place rediscovered
by those living in the West End who made day trips to see the
murder sites. 'A collective, morbid curiosity' was how their reporter
described the phenomenon. People who rarely went further than the
City drawn to a place they knew only by reputation. Drawn in by
the violent actions of a crazed killer rather than the appalling living
conditions of the area's inhabitants.

As the weeks passed, a local infamy grew into a worldwide sensation
discussed and debated in column inches and selling Whitechapel's
murders to an audience far away from London's East End quarter,
attracted by the banner headline: 'Jack the Ripper'. Fame and
notoriety on a scale unprecedented and there was more to come.

Chapter 22

Mary Jane Kelly, 9 November 1888

It is thought Mary Kelly moved into 13 Miller's Court either at the end of 1887 or early in 1888. She rented what was essentially the back room of 26 Dorset Street. It looked out on to a courtyard and was reached through a passageway separating the house from its neighbour, which was run as a chandler's shop. Both properties were owned by a man named John McCarthy who let rooms at reasonable rents. The courtyard itself, which press reports described as being roughly 30ft x 10ft (9m x 3m), was hemmed in by houses on each side whose rooms were also let, and was poorly lit. Something in common with large parts of Whitechapel, street lighting being in its infancy at that time.

None of this would have inconvenienced Mary, born in Limerick, Ireland and raised in Wales into a world that, for many, would have gone dark when the sun went down and stayed that way until dawn. The advent of street lighting, common but poor by 1888, helped illuminate the main thoroughfares but not the alleyways and sideroads she would have been familiar with. Costs were prohibitive when it came to installation, particularly in areas like Whitechapel, and were a constant barrier to change.

Having a bed for the night was more important for most of the area's inhabitants than having a well-lit street, something Mary had tried to ensure was a constant in her life by renting the room in Miller's Court under her own name, despite Joseph Barnett, her long-term partner moving in with her. Two incomes were better than one when earnings were never guaranteed. But, as it turned out, this arrangement was no proven surety long term. Barnett decided to move out after an argument over her decision to offer shelter to another woman. Space in the room at Miller's Court was not its greatest asset. Despite their disagreement, he later insisted, they remained on good terms. Nevertheless, the split possibly affected Mary's ability to pay her rent. By the start of November, she was in arrears – so much so that on 9 November John McCarthy sent his employee, Thomas Bowyer, to collect what arrears he could. The time, by his reckoning, was around a quarter to eleven in the morning. Mary was perhaps not known as an early riser and was described later by most newspapers as being 'a woman of the unfortunate class', which meant she sold sex. Therefore, late morning was a better time to start a conversation about rent owed. But when he knocked on the weather-beaten door there was no response, and the window beside the door was still covered by a makeshift curtain. To his mind she had simply overslept, and maybe that was not so unusual. So, he thrust a hand through a broken pane and moved the curtain aside, something he may well have done before. Mary was no stranger which meant he probably knew the layout of the room and that the bed was to the right of where he stood. All it needed was a quick shout out – routine stuff.

Chillingly, on this morning, there was nothing routine about trying to rouse Mary Kelly from her bed. What Bowyer saw inside that room through the narrow opening of that broken pane was truly horrific. So horrific it is unlikely he ever fully recovered from the shock. Minutes later, he was back at the window with John McCarthy in tow. Another quick lift of the curtain to convince his boss that he had not exaggerated what lay beyond was all it took to change his world forever.

Clearly shocked, understandably agitated and extremely upset by what they had seen, both men rushed to Commercial Street police station, where they confronted the desk sergeant. Duty Inspector Walter Beck probably realised from the moment they began their story he had another Ripper murder on his hands. But before he raised the alarm, and aware of what would follow when he did, he needed to confirm it for himself. If his initial assessment, based on what the two men told him, matched what he knew about the Ripper, then it warranted a high-profile response and the involvement of Scotland Yard. But there were obvious ramifications if that initial assessment was wrong. After some in-house consultation it was therefore decided to take a few constables back to Miller's Court and be certain as to the seriousness of the murder before raising the alarm level higher.

By 11 a.m., Inspector Beck was closing off both ends of Dorset Street and sending out messages for inspectors Abberline and Reid to attend. Lifting that curtain a third time was enough to convince him what lay beyond the door of Miller's Court could only be the work of one man. Officers were dispatched to spread the word and locate divisional surgeon Dr Phillips. He arrived around 11.15 a.m. After his quick visual assessment of the scene inside, and the landlord having no key to open the door, he agreed there was no urgent need to force entry. Life was clearly extinct. So, they waited for senior inspectors to arrive which took another fifteen minutes or so. There followed a further delay when it was thought bloodhounds were to be brought to the scene. Their perceived value to the Ripper investigations had obviously been discussed some days earlier, the consensus being they could prove useful, but only if the crime scene were uncontaminated. So, no attempt to break-in was made until after 1.30 p.m., when disappointing news finally arrived that there were to be no bloodhounds and therefore contamination would not be not an issue.

The scene that confronted these men as they filed in is almost indescribable and hard to comprehend even to a modern audience well used to seeing murder portrayed whether through film or TV drama. The level of carnage was beyond anything any man entering that room had ever seen. Murder and mutilation that surpassed anything Hollywood or television drama today could or would want to re-create. Mary Jane Kelly, her name of course never in doubt, had been de-humanised.

She had, in every sense, been ripped apart and displayed on the centre of the bed as a shredded corpse. A later account of the discovery described that bed as being to the right of the door, its head against the outside wall and pushed up against a partition separating her room from the one next door. The killer had worked by the light of a small candle and, probably, the light cast by the glow from a fire, the remnants of which were still in the fire-grate which was positioned opposite the door everyone had entered by.

In Dr Phillips' evidence to the later inquest, which was brief, he believed Mary Kelly had been lying on her right side, which meant she had faced the partition wall, possibly asleep, and was turned towards the middle of the bed after her right carotid artery had been cut. Blood saturated the bed, the pillow and the sheeting in the right-hand corner, which supported his hypothesis – as did the large quantity of blood that had pooled beneath the bed in the same area.

He did not, at that juncture, explain in more detail the injuries she had sustained, but the crime scene photographs are all that is needed to see the appalling injuries that were inflicted after death. Mary Jane Kelly, in every sense of the word, had been gutted. Most of the detail of how that was accomplished and just exactly how bad the mutilations were appeared in various newspapers days after the murder. However, when the inquest into Mary Kelly's death opened in Shoreditch on Monday, 12 November, the presiding coroner, Dr Roderick MacDonald, closed down the hearing before any detailed medical testimony (which was still being gathered) could be presented to the jury. This action ensured medical testimony detailing the appalling nature of the wounds inflicted on Mary Kelly was never heard in public, nor was time of death clearly established. By contrast, Coroner Wynne Baxter had always been meticulous in the level of medical detail he strived to achieve in his court, which makes MacDonald's decision to terminate when he knew that evidence was forthcoming difficult to understand. It also raises the possibility that Mary Jane Kelly's body had been taken to a mortuary under the jurisdiction of the north-eastern district coroner for just such a purpose. One has to wonder all these years later just exactly what lay behind that decision, and whether it was solely his own to make.

Either way, once made there was no going back. Of all the Ripper murders, this one, Mary Kelly, last of the canonical five, seems to have received the least publicity. No constantly adjourned coroner's court of course meant no drip, drip of information seeping into the public domain. In turn, newspapers had little new to report on and so the case slipped further into the background and out of public consciousness. Yet, by this stage of the investigation into the Whitechapel murders, press interest really ought to have been more clamorous. Police had learnt from the previous murders how to better protect and understand the murder scene. They had brought in additional medical expertise in the form of Dr Thomas Bond to enhance that of their own divisional surgeon. They had also preserved the murder site by using photography. No initial search was allowed without that photographic backup. They also had a killer profile drawn up to help in detection and re-evaluated witness evidence and how it was gathered and used. So, when police entered 13 Miller's Court that November day, they had already greatly improved their chances of catching the killer than at any other stage. One week on from the killing, despite gaps, they even had a reasonably accurate timeline for the day Mary Kelly died, garnered from people who had either known her as a neighbour or a 'name' on the street.

The start of that timeline came initially from the man who had lived with her until a few days before the murder, Joe Barnett. He confirmed in a police interview he been in the room at Miller's Court with Mary around 7.30 p.m. on the Thursday night a few hours prior to her murder, his statement corroborated by a woman named Lizzie Albrook, a friend of Mary's who called at about eight o'clock. Mary was next seen at 10 p.m. drinking in the Horn of Plenty public house in Dorset Street. Near neighbour, Mary Cox, who lived at 5 Miller's Court told police she saw Kelly with a man on the same street at around 11.45 p.m. She had followed the two of them as they made their way back to the court and saw both of them go into Mary Kelly's room.

At 2 a.m., labourer, George Hutchinson, who had walked all the way back to Whitechapel from Romford, saw her near Flower and Dean Street. She stopped him to ask if he could lend her 6d. She was out of luck. George had returned without any money, even paying for a bed for the night beyond his means. But he knew Mary, and so the two of them chatted together for a while. She then wandered off to look for someone else who could help, and that help was not far away. Hutchinson claimed he saw her minutes later in company with a man, about 5ft 6in tall, 34 or 35 years old, dark complexion and with a dark moustache turned up at the ends. The two of them walked back towards where he stood, which had allowed him to see the man more clearly, then walked on into Dorset Street. Something in what he saw, maybe the way the man was dressed – he never explained – caused him to turn back and follow. According to his story, he stayed in the shadows and watched as they paused for two or three minutes outside the entrance into Miller's Court, near enough to hear Mary say, quite loudly, 'I have lost my handkerchief.'

> He pulled a red handkerchief out of his pocket and gave it to Kelly, and they went up the court together. I went to look up the court to see if I could see them, but could not. I stood there for three-quarters of an hour to see if they came down again, but they did not, and so I went away. My suspicions were aroused by seeing the man so well dressed, but I had no suspicion he was the murderer… He was wearing a long, dark coat, trimmed with astrachan, a white collar, with black necktie, in which was affixed a horseshoe pin. He wore a pair of dark spats, with light button over boots, and displayed from his waistcoat a massive gold chain. His watchchain had a big seal with a red stone.

Best description yet of the Ripper? Or too good to be true? If what he witnessed is really true, then Hutchinson saw the killer. The results of the post-mortem examination, omitted from that inquest court, had shown Mary Jane Kelly had eaten fish and chips on the night of her death; some of it had remained in her stomach enabling Dr Bond, involved in that examination, to try and finally put a time around her murder. Given the manner of her killing this was obviously extremely difficult to do but based solely on stomach contents his best estimate of time of death is somewhere around 1 a.m. to 3 a.m. with an obvious allowance for error. Certainly, this was reasonable based on the fact that the residue of that last meal would have taken 2–3 hours to leave her stomach.

Given Hutchinson's time for Mary meeting this man it is reasonable to assume the fish and chips had been consumed prior to their meeting. It also supports the notion that he was her killer. Buying a fish supper after 2 a.m. even in Whitechapel was not so easy. But the question his sighting poses is simply why is this man so well dressed and wearing expensive finery in a notorious area of Whitechapel at that early time of the morning? Hutchinson's description makes him memorable and, therefore, unforgettable to anyone else passing him on a street. Hardly a fitting disguise for a serial killer who so far had maintained a level of anonymity in keeping with the nature of the crimes he committed. However, there can be no escaping the fact, based on the times stated, if Hutchinson's evidence really is accurate then this man did kill her. It has to be almost certain she was dead by 3 a.m., the time at which Hutchinson decided to leave the bottom of the passage that led to Mary Kelly's room. The clock on Whitechapel church, he claimed, striking the hour as he left and as he had said to police, no one else entered or left whilst he was there. Police certainly appeared to place a deal of confidence in his account. Whether this is justified may be debateable. But he had known Kelly which, perhaps, for them added to his credibility. He also knew she liked to drink but was sober when he saw her. Mary, police knew by this stage, had last taken alcohol in the Horn of Plenty some three or four hours before Hutchinson saw her, which meant she would have been sober when he saw her at 2 a.m. But what did not fit then and does not fit so easily today was how that finely crafted description failed to match any of those descriptions given by witnesses from the previous murder enquiries.

As if to highlight the point, the following 'supposed' descriptions of the Ripper were re-published by the *Wigston Advertiser* in their Saturday edition on 17 November and they make interesting reading:

> At 12.35 a.m. 30 September, with Elizabeth Stride, found murdered at one a.m., same date, in Berner Street – a man, aged 28, height 5ft 8in, complexion dark, small dark moustache: dress, black diagonal coat, hard felt hat, collar and tie; respectable appearance, carried a parcel wrapped up in a newspaper.

> At 12.45 a.m., 30th. With same woman in Berner street, a man, age about 30, height 5ft 5in, complexion fair, dark hair, small brown moustache, full-face, broad shoulders; dress, dark jacket and trousers, black cap with peak.

> At 1.35 a.m., 30 Sept, with Catherine Eddowes, in Church passage, leading to Mitre Square, where she was found murdered at 1.45 a.m., same date, a man, aged 30, height 5ft 7in or 8in, complexion fair, moustache fair, medium build; dress, pepper-and-salt colour loose jacket, grey cloth cap, with peak of the same material, reddish handkerchief tied in knot, appearance of a sailor.

Obviously, these descriptions of a possible killer are nothing like the man seen in Miller's Court, which highlights the difficulties encountered by police throughout their Ripper investigation. But there are also other relevant differences between the murder of Mary Kelly and the other murders in 1888.

Mary Jane Kelly was murdered indoors. The Ripper was a street killer. In Miller's Court he struck whilst she was asleep, nothing like that could ever have happened outside. He took no organs, or at least if he did that information was never released. The inquest was held in Shoreditch when it ought to have been in Whitechapel, and finally if the man Hutchinson saw was not the killer, then she was murdered in her sleep by a man she knew. There was only one way into 13 Miller's Court, and it was through that locked door. Mary and Joseph Barnett had lost the key some weeks earlier., but it was no inconvenience. The two of them knew how to reach in through that broken window and manipulate the door handle to release the lock; police, her landlord and apparently her neighbours did not, which supports the theory if the killer had let himself in then he must have also known the secret.

Conclusions

Clearly, there is an apparent link connecting at least four of the so-called canonical five. Mutilations carried out on Mary Ann Nichols, Annie Chapman, Catherine Eddowes and Mary Jane Kelly are sufficiently similar to suggest a common killer. Though, it has to be said, if he killed Mary Kelly, he had stepped away from what had become the accepted norm. She was killed indoors; the mutilations were more extreme and because the inquest prevented medical evidence being heard, there is doubt as to whether he took any organs away. Over the years, there has been reasoned debate over whether her heart was missing. It was not found inside her body when discovered, but then again neither was anything else. Her killer, it would appear, had been thorough in his removal of all her internal organs, using them to create a macabre, bloody display all around that tiny room in Miller's Court. Something seclusion and time had allowed him to do. Certainly, there seems to have been little speculation from the press in their reporting of the murder to suggest any suspicions had been raised by the omission of those post-mortem findings. So, there must be room for doubt.

There was no such doubt over Elizabeth Stride. The murder in Berner Street was brutal, fast, silent and expertly carried out. But no mutilation here and no attempt at any. That raises suspicions her death was not at the hands of the Ripper, although the arguments raised always declare it lacks the Ripper traits because he must have been disturbed and maybe that is the case. However, it perhaps does not fit. This murder is along similar lines to that of Frances Coles, Alice McKenzie and Rose Mylett, where murder was the only intention. Does that mean there was more than one Whitechapel killer operating throughout the 1880s and into the early nineties?

The answer to that must be yes. Whilst Jack the Ripper was operating unhindered by police so were others such as the Thames Torso killer, the West Ham murderer who took twelve young women from the streets over approximately a seven-year period: the killer of Martha Tabram, Emma Smith and Annie Yates, and the attacker of Annie Millwood and Ada Wilson. All in all, the 1880s proved itself to be a very dangerous decade and murder was more commonplace than perhaps in preceding years. So, whilst the Ripper always grabs our attention there had to have been others.

Contentious of course, particularly in the case of the Whitechapel killings, and intentionally so. But there is evidence to support the hypothesis. The police were never able to substantiate the commonly held belief of a one-man murder spree – though once the press, and public, had adopted the sobriquet 'Jack the Ripper' they were given little option. It simply became the accepted norm. But when ex-Chief Inspector Edmund Reid was interviewed by the *Leinster Advertiser* on 15 October 1913, long after his retirement, he was categoric in his belief that no one in the force, past or present, had the slightest idea of just who this Jack the Ripper character was. According to him there had been speculation from certain quarters; Sir Melville MacNaghten, Sir Robert Anderson, Dr Forbes Winslow, Sir Henry Smith, and Major Arthur Griffiths, had, he claimed, all stated they believed they knew the killer's name, but, as he rightly pointed out, had never managed to prove it. But there had been suspects, some more pertinent than others.

In late 1888, Charles Ludwig, a 40-year-old German, living at 1 The Minories, was arrested after attacking a man near a coffee stall at the corner of Commercial Road at three o'clock in the morning. According to police, during the arrest he had been found in possession of a long-bladed knife, a razor and a long-bladed pair of scissors. In the fevered atmosphere surrounding Whitechapel, that ownership alone had understandably raised his profile and rendered him a man of interest. Investigations carried out after his appearance at the magistrates' court added to that interest when it became clear he was also suspected of having attacked a prostitute in September. City Police had been looking for him in connection with a knife attack on a prostitute in the Minories. For a moment there was real, and apparently well-founded speculation, that the Ripper had been caught. He certainly fitted the profile of Whitechapel's night-time killer, as widely circulated by the press: 'respectably dressed ... about five feet six high, and wore a high silk hat'.

According to City constable John Johnston, who had responded to cries of 'murder', Ludwig and the woman he was with were in a small court, just off the Minories. The constable's initial thought was that it was simply a drunken scuffle. Ludwig appeared clearly intoxicated. No knife was in sight, and none was mentioned. That only became known after he had pulled the two of them apart and let the German go. It was too late then to effect an arrest, which was why City Police later put out an alert and released his description. It had therefore fallen to Inspector Pimley, H Division, whose force made the arrest, to investigate the man in as much detail as they could. Fortunately for Charles Ludwig, whose real name was discovered to be Wetzel, what they found was far less incriminating than initially believed. He was a hairdresser. The 'weapons' were tools of his trade. He had been living in the area for about fifteen months, spoke very little English and had nothing to do with any of the Whitechapel murders. There was no case to answer. The story fell out of favour with the press and slowly faded into obscurity.

The German connection, however, continued after *Lloyds Weekly Newspaper* ran a story in October 1888 claiming the mutilations carried out on the Ripper's victims could have been made to facilitate the making of the so-called *diebslichter* or *schiafslichter*, otherwise known as thieves' lights or soporific candles. Essentially, these were candles made in the normal way but with the inclusion of a female uterus and various other organs or parts of organs extracted from the corpse of a woman. When lit, these candles, according to German superstition, would throw out a sleep-inducing light and were much valued by anyone involved in larceny. How widespread this unlikely practice was is not known.

Nevertheless, it kept the Ripper story alive, and undoubtedly helped sell newspapers. It also added to the already growing worldwide coverage these murders were attracting by the beginning of the winter of 1888. Something that has continued up until the present day and will continue well into the future.

But who was Jack the Ripper, and did he ever stop? A question as relevant today as it was in 1888. It also raises the other question of just how many victims did he claim and was Frances Coles one of them? Certainly, for many she was the last killing he ever made and there are a few supporting factors. In the main, Jack operated in the early hours of the morning, generally between one and three o'clock and, with the exception of Mary Jane Kelly, always outdoors. The victims themselves were always classed as prostitutes though the assertion was not always borne out by the evidence uncovered and perhaps had more to do with the way Victorian society viewed women and their supposed role within it. In other words, women in straitened circumstances out on the streets in the early hours categorised as such by virtue of gender and perceived financial need. A sort of righteous dogma, endemic throughout society at that time. Nevertheless, whatever the rights or wrongs of that thought process the very act of being on those streets at that sort of hour made them vulnerable. Prey almost, to be hunted down and seemingly killed at random. But murdered in such a way that suggested a pattern, a method, a sure, well-practised and efficient killing technique. Every victim appeared to have died without a struggle. No noise, killed on the ground and by use of a knife wielded in such a way as to significantly reduce the killer's likelihood of sustaining any blood staining. In every way a silent assassin and every murder carried out as if by appointment. Frances Coles follows that same pattern or appears to. Why did she go to Swallow Gardens? It was roughly a 1-mile walk from where she met Ellen Calanna. What was so important she would go into a dark tunnel thoroughfare at two o'clock in the morning? Was it sex with a man with shiny boots? Or was it the 2-shilling pieces wrapped in newspaper and hidden behind that gutter pipe? What had been her reasoning for making that walk and had she arranged to meet someone beneath Arch 45?

In October 1896, *Lloyd's Weekly Newspaper* was again caught up in the Ripper story when it published an account of how the Whitechapel murderer operated and exactly who he was. It came from a sailor, James Brame. Son of a Lowestoft surgeon, Brame claimed to have known the killer and to have attended his funeral in April 1895.

> Mr Brame left South Shields as cook in the Annie Speer, a barque bound for Caldera, South America, in October 1894. Amongst the crew was one man who particularly attracted attention by his strange behaviour soon after the voyage commenced. He answered to the name John Anderson, was apparently about 38 years old, and was a fine, well set-up man with a bearing almost military. In complexion he was fair, his hair being red; he wore a moustache and a slight beard, and his face was much pitted with small-pox.

This man, according to Brame's newspaper account, was the Ripper; a man with a perfunctory knowledge of anatomy gained from his earlier work in the American navy where he had worked as a hospital assistant and, as reported by Brame, a man with a deep hatred of London's prostitutes. The cause of this, Brame claimed, was his ruination by one whilst living in London; a woman this man Anderson met whilst working on the ships that plied their trade between London and Rotterdam; work that allowed him to earn a regular income – possibly even enough to set money aside. How much money, Brame never explained but hinted there had been enough of it to feel its loss to who he described in his story as being, 'a low woman in London', and that loss had demanded retribution and revenge. Something Anderson, according to Brame, decided he would inflict on Whitechapel's prostitutes whenever he could, even leaving the sea for a short while to better facilitate the murders he felt it necessary to commit: '[He] took lodgings at a quiet farm-like house near Bromley, here he passed as a ship's watchman engaged at night in the docks.'

This occupation deflected suspicion from amongst his near neighbours and allowed him unfettered access into Whitechapel and the docks area. But, so the story claimed, he never worked alone. Once ashore and in the East End he would meet with a man whose job it was to help keep his identity secret. The two would work together, in plain sight, wearing smocks over their clothing after the killings to create the appearance of men employed in one of the many slaughterhouses scattered across the district.

Brame claimed to have recorded proof of this in a written statement taken down by himself after both he and Anderson had been taken off the *Annie Speer* at the port of Iquique due to illness. Anderson the worse of the two, and being near death, had confessed to being the Whitechapel murderer. Brame had written down the confession and eventually attended Anderson's funeral in April 1895. The confession was apparently lost some time later, following a shipwreck, before Brame could put it into the hands of the authorities.

Plausible, but rightly treated with some scepticism by the newspapers that later picked up the story and published it because of the Ripper connection. The notion of London's most famous murderer escaping the crime scene by sea, as already pointed out, was a popular much discussed, theory. But how true was Brame's account? Its credibility rested to some extent on its authorship. Brame was a sailor, he had been at sea throughout the early 1890s. Research shows he had served on board the SS *Golfer* as cook at the end of 1892, joining the ship in Middlesbrough. In February 1893, he discharged himself to take over the same role on board the SS *Georgia* where he stayed until June that same year. So, there could be no doubting his seagoing credentials. But what of the *Annie Speer*?

She was a barque (sail not steam), built in Dundee and launched in May 1891. The ship is very real. It had plied its trade between England and South America throughout the 1890s as Brame had claimed. According to crew lists for 1893–4, he had also been on board for one of those voyages and it had docked in the South American port of Iquique, all of which adds serious credibility to his story. But that is as far as it goes. James Brame was on board in October 1893, not 1894 as he claimed. He was not taken off because of illness, there was no other crew member named John Anderson and there was no shipwreck. In fact, he left the ship when it returned to England in July 1894 and was paid £18 10s for his work as the ship's cook. His story is pure fabrication. The ship did return to Iquique in October 1894, but he was not on board.

Had his story proven to be true, at least in the detail of Anderson being a crew member and both men being on board during the same voyage, then that would have put him in the frame for the 1888 murders and Frances Coles three years later. But like so many stories woven into the fabric of the Ripper killings throughout the 1890s, they lack key detail and fail to convince because of it. Not that it stopped these accounts from surfacing. According to a variety of newspaper reports circulating the world and picked up by the British press, Jack the Ripper was alive and well long after the East End murders had ceased. New York reported he had struck in America; Nicaragua claimed he had murdered six in ten days; Paris had its own version. So did Germany and there were even claims made of Jack killing in Vienna. Notoriety bought headlines and filled column inches.

It also brought claims of secret knowledge from various London policemen once the search for Whitechapel's serial killer had fizzled out and the century reached its close. Chief Inspector Abberline seems to have settled on Severin Klosowski, otherwise known as George Chapman, the Borough poisoner. He was executed in Wandsworth in April 1903 for the murder of three women by antimony poisoning. Though why Abberline should have thought a poisoner had also been butchering women on Whitechapel's streets remains a mystery. Ex-Chief Constable Sir Melville MacNaghten initially seemed to believe it was Montague John Druitt then changed his mind and supported the notion it could have been Aaron Kosminski. Sir Robert Anderson, Assistant Commissioner, tended to agree with him, and there were others, all of whom have been written about and discussed too many times to revisit in this text.

After James Sadler's release from the charge against him for murdering Frances Coles, the police's search for her killer, and in turn all the Ripper murders by association, simply stopped. The case remained open, arguments raged over whether or not it should be added to the Ripper file or set aside. There were no other suspects of note and had it not been for the possible connection to the murders of 1888 it would have been forgotten, consigned to history where it would have forever languished amongst the unsolved. As it is, the case sits on the fringes of the most avidly read and researched crimes in London's history and, by virtue of that close association, is never likely to slip into total obscurity. If her killer really was the man responsible for five or more of the most appalling murders the world has ever seen, then whatever name fits the suspect list must be linked to her, no matter how tenuously. Though it is doubtful the link will ever be proven.

Forbes Winslow, who, as explained in an earlier chapter, believed he knew the killer's identity at one point, would probably agree. Though it is possible he may have also entertained doubts over there ever only being five Ripper murders. As is often stated, serial killers must start somewhere and as previously outlined there were murders before Mary Nichols, not carried out with the same ferocity granted but some, if not all, could have been by the same hand, something argued in various published articles. If accepted, the concept of a canonical five could, therefore, be misleading, Certainly, for Dr Winslow, who it has to be said had no real expertise in murder only in those that committed it, there was room for debate. He clearly had reservations about Alice McKenzie but then seemed to support the idea that Martha Tabram was a victim. So, probably for him, the number of victims may well have exceeded five, though Mary Jane Kelly was the last; not because the killer had died or was in prison, but because he had left the country. This placed the Frances Coles murder outside the Ripper's reign of terror. Something he seemed to firmly believe when he gave that interview to the reporter from *The Courier* in July 1910, where he explored in more detail the Ripper's exodus from London, arguing that his account of the killer's movements published by the *New York Herald* after police had failed to follow up his lead over the murderer's Sunday morning visits to St Paul's had been pertinent, and instrumental, in his deciding to escape Whitechapel.

Remember, the Ripper, according to Forbes Winslow, had been a seaman who slipped away from London docks whenever he felt it necessary to put some distance between himself and the murders he had committed – something not too difficult to achieve given the number of ships recruiting crews on any given day of the week. Phases of the moon and a tidal river, were perhaps influential factors in the killer's decision making. But what was different about that interview with *The Courier* was not the doctor regurgitating old ideas – it's unlikely the press would have been interested had that been the case. Their reading public was all too familiar with theories and hypotheses offering nothing more than unfounded speculation which had been in circulation for over twenty years at that stage. What probably brought them to the doctor's door on this occasion was a letter; not a letter written by the supposed killer complete with smudged ink and blood stains, but a letter purporting to have verifiable information about a possible Ripper identity.

It had arrived on the doctor's doormat from an unnamed source in Melbourne, Australia. The writer, known to Dr Winslow, but not identified to the press reporter, perhaps for fear of ridicule, offered content that was both cogent and persuasive. Whether there had been previous correspondence between them or whether this was in response to something the doctor had written and published in Australia is not clear. But its author was certainly familiar with Dr Winslow's views on why the killings had stopped and was offering supportive evidence: 'Your challenge is more justified re "Jack the Ripper". You indeed frightened him away, for he sailed away in a ship called the *Murrumbidge*, working his passage to Melbourne, arriving here in the latter part of 1889.'

According to the press article, which only quoted parts of the letter, the man was a native of Melbourne, Victoria, had been educated at the 'Scottish College', and had been a friend of a local doctor (not named) who had allowed him access to post-mortem examinations before he had sailed for London. He had also married after returning to Australia, but his wife had died within a year, and he had maintained a keen interest in London newspapers, which he bought regularly. The letter writer also claimed he had closely followed the murder trial of James Canham Read and had admitted to being the Whitechapel murderer: 'I wrote to Scotland Yard telling them all. Sir Robert Anderson answered my letter, but as I had told him all I had to say, I did not write again till last year, but I have heard nothing from them.'

Whether London police ever followed this up is doubtful and though, as the reporter claims, the letter also gives the name of this Australian suspect, they did not publish it. This was 1910 and as the end of the letter suggested the man had left Australia and sailed to South Africa, so was still alive and well at the time of publication. Naming this Ripper suspect, therefore, would be problematic was he to sue. Looking at this today, it is frustrating and disappointing in equal measure. But does it stand up to scrutiny?

Well, the Scottish College is very real. Established in 1851, it is still in existence today. Also real was the much-publicised trial of James Canham Read, Jimmy to his friends, a man eventually executed for the murder of his mistress, Florence Dennis. the trial itself taking place in November 1894. The possible link between the two was that Read, up until his arrest, had been employed by the Royal Albert

Dock as a cashier. Therefore, it is quite possible the unnamed suspect in the letter and Read could well have met in the past.

This is perhaps easier to understand when you realise that the ship named the *Murrumbidge* was also very real, operating between London and Australia throughout the late 1880s and beyond. Intriguingly, the ship, under its master Arthur Pilkington, and with a crew of sixty-three, did sail from London on 1 August 1889 arriving in Melbourne just over seven weeks later on 20 September. Even more intriguing is the fact that there was, according to the ship's crew list, only one man on board who claimed to be a native of Melbourne, 20-year-old Henry J. Bride, clearly working his homeward passage to Australia because he discharged himself from the ship twenty-four hours after it docked at the Melbourne quayside, without taking discharge papers as noted in the ship's records: 'To have been signed off but did not come for his discharge', meaning he had only ever intended to sail one way and had stated that intention at the outset of the voyage.

Another intriguing point, which also creates that possible link back to Canham Read and the London shipping office, is that further checks reveal before joining the *Murrumbidge* for his voyage home, Bride had been at sea before. He was no novice sailor. On 11 April 1889, he had joined the SS *Roslin Castle*, a two-masted, steam-driven passenger liner built in 1883 and operating regularly between London and South Africa. Bride joined as an assistant steward; one of seven replacement crew taken on at Cape Town. After docking in London, and spending about four weeks in the capital, he had re-joined the same ship and set out a second time for a nine-week return voyage to the Cape of Good Hope.

None of this was unusual. It was common practice for seamen to move around different ships and leave or join at different ports. What *is* odd about Henry Bride is the fact when he joined the SS *Roslin Castle* on that first occasion back in early April 1889, he recorded on the crew list that prior to joining he had served as crew on board the *Carlisle Castle*. It was a necessary protocol, knowing a man had served before and on what ship showed his level of experience. If he had not been to sea before he was expected to sign himself as 'first ship'. Therefore, if Bride had been on the *Carlisle Castle*, as he stated there, would be a permanent record of his service.

There is not. All records pertaining to this ship and hundreds more are held at the Maritime History Archive, Newfoundland. Henry J. Bride does not appear to have served on the *Carlisle Castle* at any time between 1885–90, so why did he state that he had? Maybe he sailed from Melbourne to London on the *Carlisle Castle* not as a member of the crew but as a passenger, perhaps in early 1888. It was a passenger-carrying ship during the 1880s and made regular trips between Melbourne and London. Therefore, it is not impossible for Bride to have sailed from the southern to the northern hemisphere. If he did, then it would put him in Whitechapel at around the time of the murders; something that would add real credence to the letter Forbes Winslow had waved in the face of *The Courier's* reporter. Unfortunately, with no supporting verifiable record it is impossible to prove, and so the trail ends there. However, it does add another layer to the Ripper story and shows the letter received by the doctor was not wholly false. Its account is credible in many respects. But as the suspect's name was omitted from the *Courier's* report, Henry J. Bride's connection to the Whitechapel murders must remain speculative, however tempting that link to both London and South Africa appears to be. Intriguing though, is it not?

However, involved or not in the Ripper killings, Henry J. Bride could not have murdered Frances Coles. In 1891, he was definitely in Australia. So, the question remains – who did kill her? Having looked at the canonical five murders, Alice McKenzie and others that surround the Ripper story, clearly there are similarities in how she met her death. But is it viable to believe it was at the hands of the world's most noted serial killer? Probably not.

Looking back over the circumstances around her murder on 13 February 1891, it is plausible the police were right and the coroner's jury wrong. They brought James Thomas Sadler to court based on three key facts: one, that he had spent the night in her company, which made him culpable; two, he had sold a knife on the morning of her death; and three, he had been in the vicinity of her murder at 2.15 a.m. What let them down was their inability to place both of them beneath Arch 45 at Swallow Gardens at the same time. Yet all the evidence was there.

James Sadler, as already stated, appears deliberately vague in the statement he made to police on the morning after her death. He omitted certain facts and misplaced others in both time and place rendering nothing he stated as fact, as being easily verifiable. Obfuscation therefore, was probably his key objective and clearly it worked. Sadler's barrister, Mr Lawless, made the point in Wynne Baxter's coroner's court that no one's testimony regarding times could be trusted. All movement through Whitechapel was noted only by the chiming of a church clock or the like. The absence of personal timepieces, ensuring disparity and confusion, meant any event a witness placed in time had to be given an allowance for error – Sadler's testimony equally so. But there were some key events where that allowance could be minimised, particularly in evidence given by police officers.

On the night of the murder, Sadler had been seen by police officers around the dock area and on Tower Hill. Police officers Bogan and Westley-Edwards, two key police witnesses at the coroner's court, had seen him between 1.15 a.m. and 2.10 a.m. That last sighting left him in the vicinity of either the Minories or Swallow Gardens dependent upon the direction he chose to take. PC Edwards, the man who found Frances Coles's body beneath Arch 45 at 2.15 a.m. had confirmed the time by the Co-op clock he 'passed en route', which meant his recorded time of discovery is incorrect. A more accurate time, as stated earlier, would place his discovery at nearer 2.20 a.m. and at that point he blew his whistle. The sound of that alarm brought three other officers to the scene: Hyde, Hinton and Elliot, all of whom had run from the area in which, it has to be presumed, James Sadler must have been walking, yet no one saw him. Neither did Sadler hear the police whistle. If he had, it would have been in his statement. So where was he?

Potentially, the only other place he could have been was exiting that archway on to Chamber Street. Sore after his beating on the docks and heading towards the hospital on Whitechapel Road, Swallow Gardens was a useful shortcut. The footsteps heard by PC Ernest Edwards, therefore, were his. There was enough time, even at a slow, stumbling walk away from his encounter with Westley-Edwards, and he was a man who had already exhibited an erratic, volatile temper. Frances Coles would have stood little chance against a man of Sadler's temperament at that hour of the morning should the two of them have met. He, it must be remembered, harboured suspicions the earlier mugging had been orchestrated by her. To his mind, perhaps, payback was justified. William Fewell, porter at the London Hospital who met and treated Sadler when he eventually arrived in his casualty room, said as much in the police court. His testimony, remember, was all about treating what were minor cuts and abrasions. But when he asked about their cause Sadler had been explicit: 'The truth of it is, I have been with a woman and she has done me.'

The woman, of course, was Frances. Whether or not she was complicit in the Thrawl Street attack will never now be known but she had all the attributes that point to her involvement. She made her living on the streets. Whitechapel was her territory, it was where she made her money so her occupation alone made complicity with street gangs highly likely. Enticement was her stock in trade, and she had encouraged Sadler to spend freely whilst they were together. The pub crawl was perhaps used to ensure his vulnerability. Certainly, Sadler cannot have been the first sailor with money in his pocket to be accosted when drunk outside on a dark night and robbed. Thrawl Street even had a reputation for it which tends to support the notion Frances deliberately exposed the sailor to the potential of a street attack. Without doubt, James Sadler, from the moment he pulled himself back on to his feet, seemed to believe it true. Perhaps it even explains his truculent behaviour by the dock gate later that night. A combination of drunkenness and anger which, perhaps, had not subsided sufficiently when he walked into that archway at Swallow Gardens in the early hours of the morning.

The way Frances lay when discovered, head towards Chamber Street, feet towards Royal Mint Street, supports the hypothesis that she never saw her attacker. Certainly not clearly enough to react. There was no reported struggle. The later post-mortem identified three cuts to her throat made from two differing directions but by one killer – the significant cut being the one made by a right to left action. A clear indication surely of surprise and one inflicted by a killer stepping out in front of her. It was also the cut which put her on the ground. Any blood from the preceding wounds hit the roadway not her killer, he, most likely, only sustaining blood splatter to his hands, not his clothes. This observation is supported indirectly by William Fewell's courtroom testimony when describing James Sadler's bloody state during his hospital visit:

> I saw there was blood on his hands, and asked him if they were cut. It was some few seconds before he answered, and before doing so he put up his hands and looked at them. He then said, 'Yes, my finger is cut. He (or they) had a knife.' I looked at the finger and saw that it was only a slight cut. I then said, 'All the blood cannot come from that little cut.'

Those bloodstained hands were still in evidence later that same morning when he grabbed a cup of cocoa at around seven in the morning on Whitechapel Road. Perhaps that is what prompted him to get rid of the knife he had used to commit the murder. Evidence of the veracity of Duncan Campbell's statement to police borne out, not by the knife itself or the time of morning he bought it, but by his recollection of what Sadler said to him during its purchase. Whilst sitting in front of that roaring fire conducting the sale the sailor told him, in general conversation, about being attacked. How else would Campbell have known that fact otherwise?

Then there is the money found on him after his arrest. In total, according to police records, that amounted to £2 17s 1d and a postal order for £2. When the postal order was bought was not recorded but seems likely to have been shortly after he collected his outstanding wages of £4 15s 1d from the shipping office on the morning of Frances's death. Out of this amount he also paid his union dues in the Seamen's Union office on Tower Hill en route to the Victoria Lodging House where he remained throughout the rest of that day, only surfacing to visit the Phoenix public house in the evening and again the following morning – which is where police found him. The cost of those union fees is again not known but union dues were generally a few pennies paid weekly. He had just returned from a seven-week voyage so there would have been arrears. As for the alcohol, in 1891 it was not particularly expensive, gin cost in the region of around 4d or 5d depending on the quality of the gin. If he drank beer, then around 3d or 4d a glass. So, estimating the probable amount spent on alcohol and lodgings at around 3 shillings and adding in the 1 shilling he received for selling the knife, he ought to have had about £2 15s 4d on him when arrested.

It's obviously a rudimentary calculation and could be a little more or slightly less. Either way, it suggests he had too much cash on him when he was searched at Leman Street police station. Clearly, this was never questioned by police at the time but perhaps it ought to have been. If Ellen Calanna's evidence is accepted at face value, then after Frances went off down Whitechapel High Street with the sailor, she presumably accepted his half a crown. She was a streetwise prostitute. Payment up front would have been her mantra. If so, then where was that half-crown when her body was discovered beneath Arch 45? Was it taken by her killer, or did she stash it behind that gutter pipe? This is unlikely. Superintendent Arnold believed that money wrapped in newspaper suggested it was money to be saved or hidden – stolen goods in other words. Squirrelled away for someone else to find and that someone was probably not Frances; it is more likely that she kept any money she made. There was food to buy and lodgings to pay for. So, the absence of that half-crown on her person suggests her killer took it before he left. Was that killer James Sadler? Is that why he had more money in his pocket than he ought to have had?

Despite Calanna's evidence being regarded with suspicion by some police officers, it should in no way be discounted or classed unreliable by modern researchers. The coroner's court readily accepted her version of events whilst seeming to question that of Duncan Campbell. The story he told of buying the knife, which on the face of it is hard, verifiable fact, was more or less discarded. In turn, that means the jurors believed Frances and the well-turned-out sailor man made the walk to the Minories just as Calanna claimed. Therefore, it must also be possible that once there they made use of one of its dark courts, just as Charles Ludwig had done, then gone their separate ways. He, judging by his dress and those shiny boots, to some nearby better-quality lodging house or, as suggested earlier, the Sailors' Home, Frances towards the archway at Swallow Gardens, then on to Chamber Street, Leman Street and eventually Commercial Street and a night's lodgings.

She may have done it a thousand times, who knows? The question for police in 1891, as it is today, did James Thomas Sadler stop her?

Based on everything presented in that coroner's court, enough evidence exists to suggest he probably did. Many others will disagree, preferring to claim her as the last victim of that mysterious stranger commonly referred to as Jack the Ripper. But I believe *Jack* was long gone by February 1891.

Appendix: Statement of
James Thomas Sadler

CRIMINAL INVESTIGATION DEPARTMENT
SCOTLAND YARD

14th February 1891

James Thomas Sadler says I am a fireman and am generally known as Tom Sadler. I was discharged at 7 p.m. 11th inst. From SS *Fez*. I think I had a drink of Holland's gin at Williams Brothers at the corner of Gouldston Street. I then went at 8.30 p.m. to the Victoria Home. I then left the home and went into the Princess Alice opposite and had something to drink. I had no person with me. While in the Princess Alice between 8.30 p.m. and 9 p.m. I saw a woman (whom I had previously known) named Frances. I had known her for about eighteen months. I first met her in the Whitechapel Road and went with her to Thrawl Street, to a lodging house and I stayed with her all night having paid for a double bed at the lodging house. I don't remember the name of the lodging house where I then stayed with her. I think I then took a ship the name of which I don't remember. I did not see the woman again until I saw her in another bar of the Princess Alice and recognizing her, I beckoned her over to me. There was nobody with her. She asked me to leave the public house as when she had got a little money the customers in the public house expected her to spend it amongst them. We left the Princess Alice and went round drinking at other public houses. Among other houses I went into a house at the corner of Dorset Street, where another woman (named Annie Lawrence) joined us. This is the woman (pointing to

Annie Lawrence who was making a statement in the next office). Frances stopped me from speaking to this woman and we then went to White's Row Chamber. I paid for a double bed, and we stayed the night there. She had a bottle of whisky (half pint) which I had bought at Davis White Swan, Whitechapel. I took the bottle back yesterday and the young woman (barmaid) gave me one twopenny worth of drink for it. Frances and I left White's Row Chambers between eleven and twelve noon, and we went into a number of public houses; one of which was the Bell, Middlesex Street. We stayed there for about two hours drinking and laughing. When in the Bell she spoke to me about a hat which she had paid a shilling off a month previously. We then went on the way to the bonnet shop drinking at the public houses on the way. The shop is White's or Bakers Row, and I gave her the half a crown which was due for the hat, and she went into the shop. She came out again and said that her hat was not ready, the woman is putting some elastic on. We then went into a public house in Whites or Bakers Row, and we had more drinks. Then she went for her hat and got it and brought it to me at the public house and I made her try it on. I wanted her to throw the old one away, but she declined and pinned it on her dress. Then we went to the Marlborough Head public house in Brick Lane and had some more drink. I was then getting into drink and the landlady rather objected to Frances and me being in the house. I can't remember what the landlady said now. I heard some men in the house. I can't say their names. I had met them previously in the same house. From there I had an appointment to see a man Nichols in Spital Street, and I left her there to see Nichols, arranging to meet her again at a public house. Where I cannot say now for I have forgotten it. We came down Thrawl Street and while going down a woman with a red shawl struck me on the head and I fell down and when down I was kicked by some men around me. The men ran into the lodging houses and on getting up I found my money and my watch gone. I was then penniless, and I then had a row with Frances for I thought she might have helped me when I was down. I then left her at the corner of Thrawl Street without making any appointment that I can remember. I was downhearted at the loss of my money because I could not pay for my bed. I then went to the London Docks and applied for admission as I would go aboard the SS *Fez*. There was a stout sergeant inside the gate and a constable. They refused me admission as I was too intoxicated. I cannot remember what hour this was as I was dazed and drunk. There was a Metropolitan police officer near the gate, a young man. I abused the sergeant and constable because they refused me admission. There was some dock labourers coming out and (they) said something to me and I replied abusively and one of the labourers took it up saying. "If the [Metropolitan]policeman would turn his back, he would give me a d*** good hiding. The policeman walked across the road across Nightingale Lane towards the Tower way, and as soon as he had done so, the labourers made a dead set at me, especially the one who took my abuse. This one knocked me down and kicked me and eventually another labourer stopped him. I then turned down Nightingale Road and the labourers went up Smithfield way. I remained in Nightingale Lane for about a quarter of an hour feeling my injuries. I then went to the Victoria Lodging House in East Smithfield and applied for a bed but was refused, as I was so drunk, by the night porter, a stout fat man. I begged and prayed him to let me have a bed, but he refused. To the best of my belief, I told him I had been knocked about. He refused to give me a bed and I left and wandered about. I can't say what the time was. I went toward Dorset Street. I can't say which way, but possibly Leman Street way. When I got to Dorset Street, I went into the lodging house where I had stopped with Frances on the previous night and found her in the kitchen sitting with her head on her arms. I spoke to Frances about her hat. She appeared half dazed from drink and I asked her if she had enough money to pay the double bed with. She said she had no money and I told her I had not a farthing, but I had four pounds 15/- coming to me. I asked her if she could get trust, but she said she couldn't. I then went to the deputy and asked for a night's lodgings on the strength of the money I was to lift next day, but I was refused. I was eventually turned out by a man, and left Frances behind at the house. I then went, to the best of my belief, toward London Hospital and about the middle of Whitechapel Road a young policeman stopped me and asked where I was going as I looked in a pretty pickle. I said that I had had two doings last night, one in Spitalfields and one at the docks. I said I had been cut or hacked about with a knife or bottle. Immediately I mentioned the word knife he said, 'Oh have you a knife about you?' and there and then searched me. I told him I did not carry a knife. My shipmates, one Mat Curley another named Bowen, know that I have not carried a knife for years. The policeman helped me across the road toward the hospital gate. I spoke to the porter, but he hummed and hawed about it, and I began to abuse him. However, he did let me in, and I went into the accident ward and had the cut in my face dressed. The porter asked me if I had any place to go and I said 'No' and he let me lay down on a couch in the room where the first accidents are brought in. I can give no idea of the time I called at the hospital. When he let me out, somewhere between six and eight in the morning, I went straight to the Victoria House and begged for a few half pence, but I did not succeed, I then went to the Shipping Office, where I was paid £4 15 3d having got my money I then went to the Victoria, Upper East Smithfield and stayed there all day as I was miserable. The furthest I went out was the Phoenix about twelve doors off. I spent the night there and I was there this morning. I had gone to the Phoenix this morning to have a drink and was beckoned out and asked to come here (Leman Street) and I came.

As far as I can think it was between five and six that I was assaulted in Thrawl Street. At any rate it was getting dark, and it was some hours after that, that I went to the London Docks. I forgot to mention that Frances and I had some food at Mrs Shuttleworth's in Wentworth Street.

My discharges are as follows –

Last – discharge 11.2. 90 in London
Ship *Fez* – next discharge 6.9.90 London

Next discharge 15.7. 90 London
Next discharge 27. 5. 90 Barry
Next discharge 1. 10. 89 London
Next 2.10.88 London
Engaged 17.8.88
Next 5.5 87
Engaged 24.3.87 London

The last I had seen of the woman Frances was when I left her in the lodging house when I was turned out. The lodging house deputy can give you the time.

The clothes that I am now wearing are the only clothes I have. They are the clothes I was discharged in, and I have worn them ever since. My wife resides in the country, but I would prefer not to mention it.

The lodging house I refer to is White's Row not Dorset Street. It has a large lamp over it. Passing a little Hucksters shop at the corner of Brick Lane and Browns Lane. I purchased a pair of earrings or rather I gave her the money and she bought them. I think she gave a penny for them.

Bibliography

Anonymous, (1972) *Walter my Secret Life*

Begg, Paul, (2009) *Jack the Ripper – The Facts*

Bell, Neil R. A., (2016) *Capturing Jack the Ripper*

Bell, Neil R. A. and Wood, Adam, (2019) *Sir Howard Vincent's Police Code 1889*

British Newspaper Archive

Casebook, Jack the Ripper

Christchurch Times Saturday, 24 October 1896 – James Brame Account

Cornwell, Patricia, (2005) *Portrait of a Killer*

Eddleston, John J., (2002) *The Encyclopaedia of Executions*

Historia de la Medicina, *Iquique*

Knight, Stephen, (1984) *Jack the Ripper: The Final Solution*

Lane, Brian, (1992) *The Encyclopaedia of Forensic Science*

Maritime History Archive, – Newfoundland & Labrador Heritage

   The SS *Alford* – Crew Lists / ships records

   The SS *Georgia* – Crew Lists/ ships records

   The SS *Golfer* – Crew Lists/ ships records

   The SS *Roslin Castle* – Crew Lists 1889

   The SS *Murrumbidge* – Crew Lists 1889–1890

   The SS *Annie Speer* – Crew Lists 1895

   The *Carlisle Castle* – Crew Lists 1889–1890

Maritime Museum, *Australia Ships and Maritime History Australia*

McCreedy, Nigel, (2013) *Silent Witness – A History of Forensic Science*

Metropolitan Police Records – *National Archive: various files from MEPO3/140 including:*

   Statement of James Thomas Sadler/ Sergeant John Ward

Statement of Superintendent Arnold re Frances Coles
Statement of Thomas Fowler and Kate McCarthy
Statement of Inspector Henry Moore re Calanna/Frances Coles
  Inquest
Documents relating to Alice McKenzie / William Brodie/ Margaret
  Franklin/Sarah Sadler/Frances Coles/Sadler's arrest/Alice McKenzie
National Maritime Museum London, *C/L 978 Annie Speer (1895)*
The Salisbury Times, Saturday, 28 February 1891 – The Sadler Letter
Wade, Stephen and Gibbon Stuart, *The Crime Writers Casebook*
Wilson, Keith D., *Cause of Death – Guide to death, murder and forensic
  medicine.*
Winslow, L. Forbes, *Recollections of Forty Years.*

Index